D1601073

GARLAND STUDIES ON

THE ELDERLY IN AMERICA

edited by
STUART BRUCHEY
ALLAN NEVINS PROFESSOR EMERITUS
COLUMBIA UNIVERSITY

A GARLAND SERIES

PORTRAYING OLDER PEOPLE IN ADVERTISING

Magazine, Television, and Newspapers

THOMAS E. ROBINSON II

GARLAND PUBLISHING, Inc.
A MEMBER OF THE TAYLOR & FRANCIS GROUP
NEW YORK & LONDON / 1998

Library of Congress Cataloging-in-Publication Data

Robinson, Thomas E., 1962–
    Portraying older people in advertising : magazine, television,
and newspapers / Thomas E. Robinson II.
        p.   cm. — (Garland studies on the elderly in America)
    Includes bibliographical references and index.
    ISBN 0-8153-3215-7 (alk. paper)
    1. Aged in advertising—United States.   I. Title.   II. Series.
HF5813.U6R55 1998
659.1—dc21
                                                    98-31556

Printed on acid-free, 250-year-life paper
Manufactured in the United States of America

Dedicated to my family, Theresa, Meagan, Trey, and Charlie. Without their love and encouragement I would not have been able to devote the necessary time and effort into completing this research and my degree. I love them with all my heart and could never thank them enough for their patience, understanding, and willingness to follow me across the United States. Also, to my mother and father who always believed that I could "Do It!"

Contents

Figures

Tables and Appendices

vii

Acknowledgments

There are many people I wish to thank for contributing their time and efforts to help me complete this dissertation. I would first like to thank the five members of my dissertation and academic committee Dr. Tommy Smith, Dr. Gene Wiggins, Dr. J. T. Johnson, Dr. Mazharul Haque, and Dr. Stan Gwin.

Second, I would like to thank my buddies, good friends, and colleagues Tony DeMars and Rick Duet. With their help, friendship, and hours of collaboration I made it through the program with a smile on my face. Whenever I needed help with anything one of them was there. I look forward to working with each of them in our professional careers as we continue to strive for the TTU and LWT (the level by which all success is measured).

Finally, I would like to thank my wife, Theresa, for the many hours she gave of herself to help me earn my degree. Theresa was my secretary, coder, gopher, motivator, coach, data entry operator, slave driver, proofreader, partner, and friend. She was truly my inspiration.

Portraying Older People in Advertising

CHAPTER I

Introduction

Today's television viewer is led to believe that most "older" Americans:

—Are alike;

—Are institutionalized

—Are in poor health

—Are senile, constipated, or incontinent; and

—Are either extremely poor or very wealthy

. . . these myths and stereotypes are plain wrong.

Not only are they wrong, they convey a negative picture of aging which leads many Americans to view growing "older" with disdain and dismay. If we buy into the role models we see on television, we may begin to behave accordingly and begin to become burdens on society—not useful, productive, vital contributors.

(Horace B. Deets, 1993, Executive Director,
American Association of Retired Persons).

As society grows and changes, advertisers are faced with the challenge of matching their advertising messages to new and different target audiences. For example, children, adolescents, men, women, and "older" individuals are all audiences with specific needs, wants, and desires that advertisers must address in their advertising appeals. In addition to changing markets, advertisers are working with a media system that is continually growing and diversifying. The new media include a larger number of channels through cable and satellite systems, a variety of narrow-cast programming, the Internet, direct response television, and the increasing use of video recorders to view movies and record television shows.

One subgroup that seems to be changing and growing very rapidly is the "older" Americans, which includes those individuals 65 years or older (Bureau of Labor Statistics, 1984, as cited in Lazer & Shaw, 1987; Crispell & Frey, 1993; Doka, 1992; Linden, 1985; Lazer, 1985). At the present, older individuals represent 13% of the total United States population and it is predicted that by the year 2050 this segment will have grown to 67.5 million or over one fifth of the total United States population (See Figure 1) (Doka, 1992; Foote, 1994; Schick, 1986).

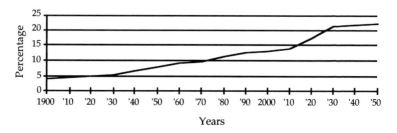

Figure 1. Actual and projected growth of the older population, 1900-2050. (U.S. Bureau of the Census, 1982 as cited in Schick, 1986; United Nations, 1991 as cited by Foote, 1994)

These figures indicate that older individuals are a large percentage of the overall population with considerable growth potential over the next 25 years. In fact, as the older population continues to grow, its members will begin to outnumber the teenagers of America by a 2-to-1 ratio (Doka, 1992). With the baby boomers reaching maturity, this group will have more income, better pensions, retire sooner, be more educated, live longer, and have better health than today's older Americans (Lazer & Shaw, 1987). Older individuals' amount of discretionary income is $1,500 to $2,100 more than the national average of $2,000 (Lazer, 1985; Lazer & Shaw, 1987). Even though some working older Americans have earnings under the poverty line, many are living well above the poverty level because they receive "80% more income than average from estates, trusts, dividends, and rentals" (Lazer & Shaw, 1987; See Figure 2).

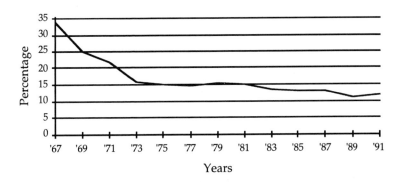

Figure 2. Percentage of individuals, 65 and older, with incomes below the poverty level. (Bureau of the Census, 1992 as cited in Foote, 1994)

When compared to the older population of 1980, older individuals in the 1990s have twice as much income (Hitschler, 1993). Americans over the age of 50 have "combined incomes of more than $800 billion, hold 51% of all discretionary income in the United States, account for 40% of consumer demand, they own almost half of the luxury cars in the country, over a third of the spa and health-club memberships, and have over three quarters of the dollars in savings" (Doka, 1992, p. 16). Also, older individuals tend to own their own homes, are mortgage free, and own 77% of all financial assets in the United States (Linden, 1985).

With the modern advancements in medicine and the information available on living a healthy life, American people are taking better care of themselves by eating healthier, exercising more, and seeing their doctors on a regular basis. This type of preventative maintenance is helping people live longer lives. For example, a male born in 1995 can expect to live to be 71 and a female to 79, but by the year 2050 the average life expectancy for males will be 74 and for females 81 years (See Figure 3).

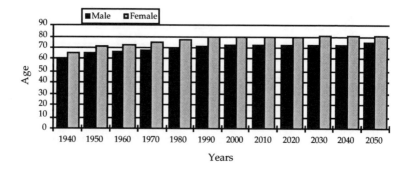

Figure 3. Life expectancy at birth and age 65 by gender and year, 1940-2050. (Social Security Administration, Social Security Area Population Projections, 1984 as cited in Schick, 1986)

According to the Social Security Area Population Projections (as cited in Schick, 1986) older individuals who reach the age of 65 can expect to expand their lives by 15 to 20 years (See Figure 4). Because of these increased life spans people aged 65 and older are no longer entering "old" age but are now experiencing a "second or prolonged middle-age" (Deets, 1993). These seniors are not in nursing homes, afflicted with Alzheimer's, or sitting around waiting to die. Deets (1993) describes today's older individuals as "active, alert, and full of vitality. They want to contribute to society and enjoy life—and, they are doing it" (p. 135).

With their strong economic base, growth potential, and life expectancy, targeting the older consumer would seem ideal for advertisers, especially when one considers that the older market accounts for 40% of the consumer demand in America (Doka, 1992). Schreiber and Boyd (1980) report that "69% of older individuals say that commercials are often or always helpful to them in making their purchase decisions and 63% believe that commercials provide them with useful information" (pp. 63-64). Additionally, Milliman and Erffmeyer (1990) reported that Hanson (1987) found in his research that "75% of the older individuals switch brands and experiment with new products" (p. 31).

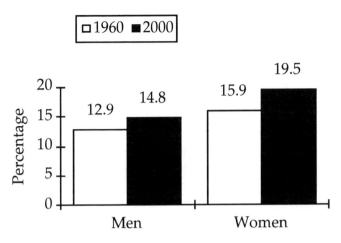

Figure 4. Life expectancy at age 65 by gender in the years 1960 and 2000. (Social Security Administration, Social security Area Population Projections, 1984 as cited in Schick, 1986; Healthy People 2000, 1992)

Because many older individuals are free from the financial burdens associated with raising children, mortgages, and furnishing a home, they are able to spend their money on themselves. Their discretionary incomes, active lifestyles, and available time make them the ideal market for "travel, leisure activities, vacation homes, time-sharing arrangements, personal-care products and services, leisure clothing, hobbies, sporting activities, self-improvement activities, cultural events, wide variety of clubs and associations, and active participation in community and nonprofit organizations" (Lazer, 1985, p. 48). Today, however, there is little evidence that advertisers and product manufacturers are targeting older Americans.

Milliman and Erffmeyer (1990) speculate that the reason many advertisers do not design advertisements specifically for the older market is because they do not know how to communicate with them. These researchers also believe that marketers do not understand older individuals' needs, wants, and desires enough to direct products or advertising to them. Some companies, however, have recognized the potential of the older market and have created a number of sales, programs, and promotions designed to attract the attention of the older consumer. For example, Royal Cruise Lines, American Express, General Foods, AT&T, Coca Cola, Subaru, Wal-Mart and McDonald's have all developed advertising and sales promotions targeting the older demographic (Konrad & DeGeorge, 1989; Castro, 1989). In addition, senior citizen discounts at restaurants and department stores, apparel designed specifically for the mature individual, and using older employees as greeters are other ways the senior market is being targeted (Lumpkin & Hite, 1988). Still, this kind of targeting is limited, and as Gerbner, Gross, Signorielli, and Morgan (1980) have observed, older Americans are underrepresented and usually stereotyped (e.g., sick, institutionalized, angry, confused, etc.) in advertising. This study, therefore, will explore the level to which selected older Americans are targeted, represented, and portrayed in general interest media advertising.

PURPOSE OF THE STUDY

The general purpose of this research is to determine the degree to which certain advertisements in the general interest media portray older individuals differently depending on the target audience. Specifically, this study examines advertisers' attempts, in the electronic and print media, to target and attract the business of the older population.

Magazines, newspapers, and television were selected because researchers have determined them to be widely used by older consumers. For example, older individuals watch more television than any other audience segment (Bell, 1992; Schick, 1986; Schreiber & Boyd, 1980); they are the largest regular readers of newspapers (Newspaper Advertising Bureau, as cited in Schick, 1986); they use newspapers most often for gathering information (Schreiber & Boyd, 1980); and they are large readers of magazines (Simmons, 1994). The major goal of this study, therefore, is to provide information to the general public, aging councils, advertisers marketing products and services to older Americans, and advertising agencies about the representation of the older audience, their portrayal, and if any stereotyping exists so that more insightful advertising can be provided.

RESEARCH QUESTIONS

Because much information could be gathered about the portrayal of older individuals in targeted and nontargeted advertisements the following research questions have been determined to guide this research:

RQ1: Is the number of older individuals appearing in selected advertisements less than their actual number of the population?

RQ2: What number of selected advertisements in the electronic and print media target older individuals?

RQ3: Are advertisements targeting older individuals related to their health (e.g., life insurance, vitamins, medicines, etc.)?

RQ4: Do advertisements targeting the older market portray the older characters in a positive manner?

RQ5: Do advertisements targeting the "younger" audiences portray the older characters in a stereotypical manner (e.g., senile, poor health, etc.).

RQ6: Do advertisements targeting older individuals show the older characters in a home setting?

RQ7: Is there a difference in the overall portrayal of older individuals in the selected media?

By determining the portrayal of older individuals in targeted and nontargeted general interest media advertisements a better understanding of how the older demographic is presented and how their business is attracted will be established.

JUSTIFICATION OF STUDY

These days the "credo in advertising is that 18-49 rules" (Taylor, 1995, p. 40). This market segment is attractive to marketers because it represents a large number of individuals who are making changes, trying new products, and spending their money. Mike Neavill, director of corporate advertising for AT&T explains:

> Advertisers identify a target audience they believe serve as the best prospect for the products or services that they have to sell. If you are selling a Cadillac, you certainly are looking for people who have a lot of purchasing power, and that tends to skew older. Our services skew younger: 18-49. Younger audiences tend to be more mobile, they're changing addresses frequently, and they have more opportunities to sign up with long-distance companies. Older audiences don't make as many physical moves; they're more loyal in their preferences. (Taylor, 1995, p. 42)

Some advertisers, such as Hal Margolis, vice president for the Lintas: Campbell-Ewald advertising agency in New York City, admits that for years no one in the advertising business has concentrated on the over-49 age group (Castro, 1989). Meanwhile, as Taylor (1995) states "the 50 plus population–the population with the most money to spend–is growing more rapidly than the 18-34 population; and the first baby boomers start hitting the half-century mark next year" (p. 40).

In advertising, the words "young" and "younger" are consistently used, while "old" and "older" are seldom referred to at all (Davis & Davis, 1985). Certain products such as beauty aids (e.g., Revlon & Oil of Olay) are made to make people feel younger with youthful advertising appeals. Davis and Davis (1985) observed that even when a middle-aged or older model is used, the copy in the advertisement still states promises of "looking" or "feeling younger." Commercials are where the promises of youth are made and older individuals are not invited to participate, "younger women sell beauty products—older women sell digestion aids, laxatives, denture fixtures, and arthritis remedies" (Davis & Davis, 1985, p. 54).

The 18 to 49 age demographic is also important to television executives because they are the main target audience for advertising (Taylor, 1995). Seligson (1993) cites an ABC executive who stated that "they (ABC) do not sell one single dollar of advertising based on reaching viewers over the age of 49." The founding president of Fox Broadcasting Company said recently, "We don't need anyone over 50 years of age to succeed with our business plan" (p. 44). Even CBS, who has been known for catering to the mature audience, is changing its programming to attract a younger audience. David Poltrack, CBS's executive vice president for planning and research said,

> We at CBS have been frustrated after years and years of trying to sell an older audience to our advertisers–and after $2 million in research disproving the myths about that audience. The advertising community is incredibly resistant to recognizing that audience (50+). The fact is that a smaller, younger audience can generate more advertising dollars, and we rely on ad dollars alone as a source of revenue (Taylor, 1995).

Indeed, advertising agency personnel and business executives do not believe the older market is important to their business, so they simply choose to leave them out of their marketing plans and advertising. The statistics and financial reports on older Americans, however, indicate that marketers and advertisers are ignoring a group with large numbers and a strong buying power (Doka, 1992; Foote, 1994; Lazer, 1985; Lazer & Shaw, 1987; Schick, 1986).

A number of articles have been published in national magazines during the past few years making claims that merchandisers and marketers are beginning to recognize and target the older market (Castro, 1989; Doka, 1992; Konrad & DeGeorge, 1989; Lehrer, 1991; Shaw, 1993). Companies such as Quaker Oats, McDonald's, Coca-Cola, and Milk of Magnesia are using older people as spokespeople (Castro, 1989). In addition, Eastern Airlines, Toyota, and Bud Light are using older actors in their advertisements (Castro, 1989).

The fashion industry is creating classical stylish clothing for those working women aged 55 to 64 and casual clothes geared toward the leisure pursuits enjoyed by retirees (Lehrer, 1991). Konrad and DeGeorge (1989) report that a number of companies, such as AT&T, Sharp Electronics, General Foods, Travelers, and Beecham Products USA, are creating products and advertising campaigns specifically for the older market. Also, Winnebago Industries, Monaco Coach, Carnival Cruise, Royal Caribbean Cruises, and Brunswick are targeting the business of the "woofie," (well-off old folks) (Wyatt, 1995, p. 131). This type of marketing is, however, infrequent and a cause for concern for some older individuals including Horace B. Deets (1993), Executive Director of the AARP, who is troubled about the lack of attention the media give the older market. Therefore, this research will help determine the extent to which the older market is being targeted in the media.

Closely related to targeting is the problem of stereotyping. For years, stereotyping older individuals as "cranky," "sick," "decrepit," "dysfunctional," "rigid," "declined intelligence," "senile," or "institutionalized" were common in television and advertising (Davis & Davis, 1985). Because of these stereotypes, older people have been used in humorous and health care-related advertising. Clara Peller gained national attention as a Wendy's spokesperson in a famous television commercial by asking, "Where's the beef?" More recently, in an advertisement for the "Medical Alert" paging device, an older woman was shown on the bathroom floor calling out, "Help! I've fallen and I can't get up." Some advertisers, like Pepsi, have continued to use this stereotypical role of older individuals to advertise their products. A good example is when Coke is delivered to the fraternity house by mistake and the Pepsi arrives at the retirement home. The advertisement shows that just by drinking Coke, young fraternity members act like old people sitting around playing checkers, reading books, moving very slowly, and being extremely boring.

Other advertising roles stereotype older individuals as "half-deaf codgers, meddling biddies, grandfatherly or grandmotherly authority figures, or sufferers in need of laxatives, denture adhesives, or sleeping pills" (Abrams, 1981, p. 37). According to Davis and Davis (1985),

> The most common role for the elderly in advertising is that of an advice giver. Because of their age, elderly individuals are called on to provide reliability to a product and enhance a sales message. These roles tend to go to male celebrities who provide a certain amount of credibility to a product. Again the stereotype is that only the elderly have the experience to recommend a product. (p. 53)

The sentiment among advertisers is that if they are not targeting a particular demographic group then why should they care how that group is portrayed. The problem then becomes one of ethics. Advertisers have an ethical obligation to be sensitive in their portrayal of specific types of people in their advertisements" (Belch & Belch, 1995, p. 694). If the older population is stereotyped, underrepresented, or excluded from advertisements targeted to younger audiences then what impression will they have of older people? Even more important, when older people watch their own portrayal in these advertisements what type of image do they develop of themselves?

One problem that may exist from a negative portrayal of older individuals in advertisements is the shaping or "cultivating" of the viewers. Gerbner, Gross, Morgan, and Signorielli (1994) have developed the idea of "cultivation" to describe to contribution the media (e.g., television) have on the viewer and their view of social reality. For example, heavy viewers of television tend to see the world like the world that is presented on television. Today, the media surround our lives, children are growing up with and are influenced by television every day and older individuals are the largest users of television (Bell, 1992; Schick, 1986; Schreiber & Boyd, 1980). Gerbner et al. have suggested that growing up with the images on television and being a heavy television user will allow for the formation of thoughts and ideas that influence later decisions. The negative portrayals of older individuals in advertising may have a lasting effect on younger and older people in society. The present research does not attempt to test the cultivation of these images but will suggest future research in this area.

The present research, therefore, concentrates on understanding how older individuals are portrayed in advertisements targeting them and advertisements targeting other demographic segments. From this research a better understanding about the ethics of stereotyping, the image younger audiences have of older individuals, and the image older individuals have of themselves will be provided.

CHAPTER II
Review of Literature

The following selected articles on past research conducted on the older audience, the older consumer, and older individuals' portrayal in advertising are presented in a topical order. The first section contains articles that discuss older individuals' portrayal on television programs. The second section reviews studies on older individuals' portrayal in magazine advertisements. The third section will review studies on older individuals' portrayals in television commercials. Finally, section four examines older individuals' appraisal of their image in advertising. Each begins with a brief description of the study's purpose, an examination of the methodology, and a discussion of the results and conclusions.

OLDER INDIVIDUALS ON TELEVISION

In an attempt to describe "age" in the world of television Northcott (1975) conducted a content analysis of drama shows broadcast during prime time on the three network channels (1) ABC, 2) CBS, and 3) NBC). Each network was monitored for one week providing a total of 41 programs or 35 hours of television programming. All role portrayals lasting more than two minutes were analyzed concentrating specifically on older characters' age, occupation, sex, race, ethnicity, social role, dramatic role (major or minor character), physical state, mental state, and living situation.

Northcott (1975), analyzed 464 roles of which only seven or 1.5% were judged to be over 64 years of age. The majority of the seven roles (5) were minor roles and the other two were major roles. Older males were shown nearly three times as often as older females. Two of the older characters were described in negative terms such as tottering, nosy, and silly gossips while the others were portrayed more positively with good health and active lifestyles. Stereotypical problems associated with older individuals such as poor health, senility, poverty, and hospitalization were not seen in the character portrayals. The older characters usually lived with someone and none were shown as being institutionalized. The findings did indicate that older people along with the very young suffer most of the problems on television. In these cases, the competent adult male is called in to solve the problem.

The results in this study indicate that older characters in prime-time dramas are represented infrequently and when they are given a role in a dramatic program it is usually a minor role and they are the ones with the problem. Only two of the seven roles analyzed were major which may represent a feeling of society nearly 20 years ago, that older people did not have a major role in what goes on in the world. Today, this trend is changing with more leading roles and characters being played by older individuals (i.e., *Murder She Wrote* and *Matlock*). Older characters were shown positively in their roles and not with the stereotypical problems they have continue to have throughout the years. Northcott (1975) did examine the portrayal and personality characteristics of the older characters; however the small number of roles (7) for the older characters provided only a limited amount of information. To better understand the portrayal of older characters on television, a larger number of characters need to be analyzed.

To extend Northcott's (1975) study beyond prime time, Harris and Feinberg (1977) examined older individuals in television programs during several different time segments and categories. Their categories included 1) prime time, 2) commercials, 3) news, 4) game shows, 5) comedies, and 6) children's programs. A four-hour random sampling of each of four time segments was selected for evaluation. All characters that appeared were evaluated as to their gender, age, levels of romantic involvement, physical activity, health problems, authority, and esteem by others. Coders observed and rated a total of 312 characters, of which 184 were between the ages of 30 and 60, 24 were ages 60 to 70 years, and only 2 were over 70 years of age.

When the characters are broken down by program category, older men and women account for 7% of the game show contestants, 6% of the drama and soap opera characters, and 9.5% of the comedy show characters. About 10% of the characters on news programs and in children's programs were over 60 years old. There was only one positive romantic involvement in individuals in the 50 to 60 category and no romantic involvement was found in characters over the age of 60. The authors do, however, note that characters over 60 are often shown in married situations but never were the loving or sexual element of that relationship an issue. Physical activity was shown to decline with age yet 14% of the 50 to 60 age group and 12.5% of the 60 to 70 age group were shown as being healthy and active. When authority and esteem by other were examined, the authors found that as age increases over 40, authority also increases for men and decreases for women. Ninety-two percent of the authority holders in the 60 to 70 age group where male. Older characters also had more health problems than younger characters. In the 50 to 60 age group 14% (9) of the 64 characters showed health problems and in the 60 to 70 age group 25% (6) of the 24 characters had poor health. These numbers do not seem high until they are compared to the 6% of all characters under the age of 50 who were shown with poor health.

Harris and Feinberg (1977) also examined 80 commercials with a total of 198 characters evaluating them on gender, age, physical activity, health problems, and authority. People over the age of 60 represented 10.6% of all the characters in commercials and there were more older males in commercials than older females. Physical activity in commercials also declined with age yet no characters were shown incapacitated or debilitated. Old people in commercials have the majority of ailments (35% in ages 60 to 70) and health problems are shown to increase with age. There were more people in commercials with poor health as compared to the programs, but this was expected because pain and illness remedies are advertised in commercials. Authority in commercials increased with age for males but as females increased in age they lost much of their authority. Men represent 68% of the advice givers in the 60 to 70 age group but in the 20 to 30 age group men account for only 12.5% of the advice givers. Celebrities were the predominant advice givers in the older age groups and twice as many of the celebrities were male than female. Advertisers will use an older model that is a celebrity to provide authority to the product but they do not trust an older noncelebrity with the same responsibility.

Harris and Feinberg (1977) found that older characters are portrayed more often in the different areas of programming than Northcott (1975) found in prime time. Comedies, news programs, and children's shows have a percentage of older characters that is more representative to their real numbers (12% in 1977) (Foote, 1994).

Romance was excluded from the older characters' lives, which adds to the stereotype that older people are not sexual. Many of the older characters were shown as healthy and active even when there was an obvious decline in activity as age increased. Most older people were shown as healthy but the results indicate that when the characters do have a medical problem they are normally older. The one area of concern from this study was the authority level of older females. Older males' authority levels increase with age but the older female loses her authority almost to the point of having no authority in television programs.

In addition to looking at programming content, Harris and Feinberg's (1977) examination of television commercials of nearly 20 years ago provides some interesting results. Older character represented 10.6% of all characters in commercials which is more closely related to their real life numbers (12% in 1977) (Foote, 1994) and better than the findings in more recent studies (Swayne & Greco, 1987, Robinson, Duet, & Smith, 1994). Other findings that were similar to more recent studies were that physical activity was shown to decline with age, older people suffered more from poor health, and male actors were given more authoritative roles. Harris and Feinberg completed one of the first examinations of the older characters' portrayal in advertising with results indicating the need for changes in the way older people are represented. The study did not, however, divide the advertisements into areas of targeting to provide information on how the older characters were shown when they were the target market for the advertisement.

In another study designed to find out what kind of images of the aged were being imported to other countries, Shinar, Tomer, and Biber (1980) looked at how older characters are presented on television programs received in Israel. Since many television programs produced in the United States and parts of Europe are broadcast in other parts of the world, the characters on these programs, which come from a particular culture, can have some influence on how other cultures view the citizens of that country. In their content analysis, a total of 562 characters were analyzed from 46 dramatic programs form a total of 56 hours from a single television channel in Israel. The programs were imported from the United States (37), England (7), and France (2). Coders looked at individual and social attributes, demographic characteristics, and the age of each character.

The results of the content analysis indicated that older people (60 years and older) represented 9.6% of the characters. This percentage is a little lower than the actual older population in the United States, but is close to the 10% older Israeli population. Most of the of major roles were held by young adults and only 24.1% of the older characters had major roles and females constituted only 18.5% of the older characters. The majority of older characters were judged as being in the middle and upper socioeconomic class and two thirds of the older characters worked in professional or executive positions or as small business owners.

To determine how the characters were presented in the programs, Shinar et al. (1980) coded the characters' attributes that were either "positive," "neutral," or "negative" (pp. 51-52). Using 64 bipolar attributes on a five-step scale, "according to the method used by Rosencranz and McNevin (1969)," they found that older characters had a 23.6% positive attribute rating, a 10.9% neutral rating, and a 65.4% negative rating (Shinar et al., 1980, p. 51). The list of negative attributes included "lived in the past," "unclean or unorderly," "prejudiced," "conservative," "physically ill," "mentally ill," "ugly," "mean," "passive," or "not contributors to society" (p. 51). On most comparisons the older characters rated well below the younger characters.

Shinar et al. 's (1980) findings support the idea that television programs contain a negative stereotype of age and older characters. Their comparison to other age groups provides support that television broadcasters in the 1970s and 1980s were interested in the younger audience and a positive portrayal of this group. The authors, however, did not mention the effect these portrayals have on Israel's view of the other countries. A survey of Israeli viewers should have been added to the results to provide information on the effects of these negative images of old people that are used in television. Overall, the results support the findings in other studies that older characters are seldom used and when they are they are shown in negative stereotypes.

In comparison to the Northcott (1975), Harris and Feinberg (1977), and Shinar et al. (1980) studies, Bell (1992) was interested in finding out if the image of older people on television had changed throughout the years, and if it had, in what direction. A content analysis was conducted on five prime time network television programs (4 dramas and 1 sitcom) which were determined to be the most popular television programs for the 55 and older audience segment since 1989. The programs were 1) *Murder She Wrote*, 2) *Golden Girls*, 3) *Matlock*, 4) *Jake and the Fat Man*, and 5) *In the Heat of the Night*. To measure the character presentation, Bell (1992) used the title sequence from each of the programs. The title sequences lasted approximately one minute as the characters are introduced and the show's setting is established.

The significance of each character in a show can be, according to Bell (1992), "measured by the number of times they appear, their total time of appearance in the title sequence, and especially by their personal credit shot, which displays the name of the actor as a graphic under the image of the character, usually in a bust shot" (p. 307). For example, on *Matlock*, Andy Griffith's credit shot states "STARRING/andy griffith" and lasts 5.08 seconds while a costar has only his or her name (no "starring") with his or her image for only 3 seconds (Bell, 1992 p. 307). The title sequence only provides visual images of the character while the show's theme song is being played. Bell claims that the title sequence and theme song combined create, for the viewer, an image of the show and characters that is true to the portrayals in the show.

Bell's (1992) analysis of the title sequences provides eight interrelated generalizations about the older characters of these shows. The first generalization is that the older characters are the center of the program. For example, on *Matlock*, Matlock's face is frozen on the screen in one corner during many of the shots indicating his central role in the show. The central nature of these older characters means as Bell states, "The audience can identify these shows with the elderly and look forward to the active participation of characters they may empathize with or see as role models" (p. 308). The second generalization in these programs is the concept of power. The older characters on these shows are powerful members of their communities and perform jobs that help the well being of those they come in contact with. In many of the shows the supporting cast members report directly to the older character that is in charge or the boss.

The third generalization according to Bell (1992), stated that the older characters in these programs are affluent as seen in their dress, place of residence, activities they participate in, and their roles. Fourth, the older characters are always healthy and are physically and socially active. In the title sequences, the Golden Girls are shown as an extremely active group, Matlock is seen standing and waving his arms in the courtroom, and Jessica Fletcher is always traveling in addition to riding a bike, jogging, fishing, investigating crimes, and writing novels. Besides being physically active, the fifth generalization concludes that each of the older characters is seen as mentally active. The roles in each of these programs include some intellectual roles such as a murder investigator, trial lawyer, police chief, schoolteacher and volunteer in a number of social activities. Additionally, the quick wittedness and good humor of many of the characters provides evidence of very active, bright, and alert minds.

Bell's (1992) sixth generalization found in each of the programs is that the characters are all looked up to and admired. In many cases their positions of authority command respect, but each also has a likable quality that draws the viewer in and engenders a feeling of admiration. The seventh generalization is that in the title sequences sexuality is generally removed from the lives of all of the older characters. The characters on these programs are regarded as being sexy (i.e., attractive, titillating, alluring) but never sexual. Finally, the eighth generalization is that the setting of each of the programs is in a somewhat protected and safe environment. The settings of Atlanta, Georgia (*Matlock*); Sparta, Mississippi (*In the Heat of the Night*); a retirement area in Miami (*Golden Girls*); and New England (*Murder She Wrote*) indicate that crime is contained yet fun and excitement can be found. Each of these settings also hold the essential value of "old patriarchy" that cities like New York, Chicago, and Los Angeles never could (Bell, 1992, p. 309).

Bell (1992) believes that the older character has become more prominent on prime-time television and that the characters are shown more positively than in the past (Harris & Feinberg, 1977; Northcott, 1975; Shinar et al., 1980). There are more strong independent roles for older women yet when women work with men as in *Matlock* and *In the Heat of the Night* they are shown as more secondary. Bell's use of the title sequence is an interesting method for evaluating the role of the older character, yet his evaluations of the programs and characters appear to coincide with the actual program content. This study provides some support, however, that older characters are receiving more major roles and roles that show them in a positive, active manner

The one area of programming where a positive and well-represented group of older individuals was consistently found was in daytime serial dramas. Cassata, Anderson, and Skill (1980) conducted a content analysis for the purpose of determining the portrayal of older adults in soap operas. Coders watched 10 episodes of a series and identified all older individuals (55 years of age and older) based on the following characteristics: "1) the eldest of at least three generations, 2) a grandparent, 3) a resident of an institution for the aged, and/or 4) a retired person" (Cassata et al., 1980, p. 48)

Cassata et al. (1980) found that of the 365 characters in the soap operas 58 (15.9%) were judged to be 55 years or older (43% in their 50s, 5% in their 60s, and 2% in their 80s). The gender of the characters was equally divided with 51.7% male and 48.3% female. Most older characters (24 of the 58) were widowed, 92.9% were shown as healthy and 75% lived in their own home either alone, with a spouse, or their children. Older females were cast mostly as homemakers or in a service or clerical position while older males were cast as professionals or managers. The majority of older characters (51%) were in the upper-middle or wealthy economic class.

The appearance of the older characters on the programs was also very positive. Ninety-eight percent were judged as "pleasant" with a positive appearance and demeanor (Cassata, Anderson, & Skill, 1980, p. 48). Their weight and dress style was also positive and acceptable. Cassata, Anderson, and Skill (1980) conclude by stating that the profile of older people in soap operas is "one of an attractive individual, usually employed in an important position, lives independently and makes up an important part of the soap opera world" (p. 49).

The portrayal of older characters in soap operas was overall the most positive portrayal on television. Older people representation in soap operas (15.9%) is more closely correlated to their real-life numbers (13%) than any other type of programming (Bell, 1992; Harris & Feinberg, 1977; Northcott, 1975; Shinar et al., 1980). In addition to their numbers, older individuals are shown in very positive roles and situations which again separates them from others types of programming. The division between the gender is nearly a 50/50 split. A very high percentage for older females when compared to other types of television programming. The daytime serial drama is, however, a unique genre that centers around a small number of families which may explain the positive portrayal of age. These family situation often have a patriarch or matriarch that is held in high regard by the other family members. Additionally, the older characters are actors who have been with the series for a long period of time and may have the respect of the producers and writers.

OLDER INDIVIDUALS IN MAGAZINE ADVERTISING

To assess the portrayal of older individuals in prescription drug advertisements, Smith (1976) developed a content analysis to examine the advertisements in two medical journals. Every advertisement in the 1974 issues of the *Medical Economics* and *Geriatrics* journals were used in the study. The coders were instructed to gather information such as gender, race, and level of activity on all individuals judged to be over the age of 60. Coders were also asked to record any assertions made about age or older people from the advertisements' copy headlines and body. Additionally, all descriptive words and phrases about older people appearing in the advertisements were recorded.

A total of 132 older individuals were detected in the two journals. Male characters were shown in a slight majority (58%) which is, as Smith describes, "still high when one considers the population normally seen by a physician" (p. 331). The race of the characters was predominately white (131 of the 132). The level of activity of the models in the advertisements were shown as active at leisure (36%), active at home (21%), disabled but functional (16%), disabled and not functional (11%), productive on the job (9%), and inactive (9%). The assertions made about older individuals in the headlines and body and descriptive words or phrases found in the advertisements provided some very negative results. From a total of 97 assertions made about age, 68 were negative and 29 were positive. A total of 111 descriptive words or phrases describing old people were detected and 74 were negative and 37 were positive.

Smith (1976) found that when older individuals were portrayed in prescription drug advertisements they were pictured as healthy, active, and in a positive manner. The copy in the advertisements, which described older people, however, was generally negative using terms such as "aimless, apathetic, debilitated, disruptive, hypochondriac, insecure, insatiable need for reassurance, low self-esteem, out of control, sluggish, reclusive, and temperamental" (p. 333). The race of the character in the advertisements was nearly all white which may reflect the time period of this study. The information this study seeks to discover should indicate if improvements in the use of minorities in advertising have been made.

In his review of literature, Smith (1976) cites McTavish (1971) who comments on the perception of the aged:

Stereotyped views of the elderly uncovered in various studies include
views that old people are generally ill, tired, not sexually interested,
mentally slower, forgetful, and less able to learn new things, grouchy,
withdrawn, feeling sorry for themselves, less likely to participate in
activities (except perhaps religion), isolated, in the least happy or
fortunate time of life, unproductive, and defensive in various
combinations and with varying emphases. (p. 333)

Smith's results show that these views also existed in the prescription
drug advertisements of 1976. Even though this study was conducted 20
years ago, many of these same stereotypes exist in advertising today. In
addition to the portrayal of older people, Smith states a concern that
physicians' attitudes toward older individuals may be reflected in or
shaped by the stereotypes in these advertisements.

Smith (1976) use of only two different medical journals may have
limited his sample and the number of older people in the
advertisements. No information was provided about the journals and
the type of medical information the journals contained or the type of
physician they targeted. The title *Geriatrics* does suggest that the
journal contained information on the treatment of older individuals.
Older individuals' characteristics and setting were examined in this
study, but their role (e.g., major, minor, or background) and placement
with others in the advertisement was not discussed.

In addition to research conducted using medical journals, a number
of studies have been designed to determine how older people are
portrayed in the advertisements of general interest magazines. One
study by Gantz, Gartenberg, and Rainbow (1980) examined how older
individuals are portrayed in magazine advertisements and how
frequently they appeared in advertisements featuring people. Seven
national magazines were selected (1) *People*, 2) *Reader's Digest*, 3)
Time, 4) *Sports Illustrated*, 5) *Ladies' Home Journal*, 6) *Playboy*, and
7) *Ms.*) for the study. According to the authors, these magazines
represented a "broad spectrum of genres and a large mass circulation"
(p. 56). Every issue from each magazine for the year 1977 was coded
and analyzed for a total of 6,785 advertisements containing people. To
determine the older models from the other individuals in the
advertisements, the researchers used the following criteria to define an
older person: "1) direct mention of age, 2) extensive gray hair, 3)
wrinkling of the skin, 4) use of a cane, crutches, or wheel chair, 5) a

reference of grandmother or grandfather, and 6) a reference to being retired" (p. 57).

From their content analysis, Gantz et al. (1980) determined that 5.9% of the advertisements in the magazines contained at least one older person. There were a total of 17,838 people and only 551 (3.1%) were older, clearly providing evidence that older characters are underrepresented in magazine advertising. When older individuals were placed in an advertisement, the number of total people in the advertisement increased to an average of 4.0 people while advertisements without an older character contained an average of 2.5 people. Placing others around the aged may be a direct reflection of advertisers' lack of confidence in this market. Older people did advertise a wide variety of products and their most popular role being the corporate image (14.4% of the advertisements containing an older person). The majority of older people in advertisements were male indicating that there is even less representation of the older female whose life expectancy is much greater than a male's. There was no great difference in the products that older men or older women advertised. The underrepresentation of the older population means, as Gantz et al. points out, that advertisers do not see the older consumer as major players in the marketplace.

The Gantz (1980) study provides valuable information on the portrayal of older people in advertisements and their underrepresentation in national magazines. The only real problem with this study was the researchers' choice of magazines to analyze. Because the authors' reasons for selection were to have magazines with a large readership and a variety of genres, choosing the magazines they did is understandable. Magazines such as *Playboy* (whose target market is males 18 to 43 years old), *Sports Illustrated* (whose target market is males 18 to 34 years old), and *Ms.* (whose target market is females 18 to 34 years old), however, are targeted at very specific age demographic segments and they do not have high readership with adult or senior audiences (Simmons, 1994). Selecting magazines with a more general appeal and a larger adult and senior readership may have provided more valuable results. Also, the authors did not look at any possible differences in older individuals' portrayal in advertisements targeted at the older market or those targeted at a younger audience. Providing this information would have been helpful in understanding the portrayal of older individuals.

To determine if the use and portrayal of older individuals had changed throughout the years, Ursic, Ursic, and Ursic (1986) examined magazine advertisements from 1950 to 1980. The authors selected their magazines based on nine different topic categories listed in Standard Rate and Data Service, a circulation over 500,000, an initial publication date before 1950, and a broad appeal to the general readership of the topic category. The nine categories with their corresponding magazines were as follows: "Science," *Scientific American*; "Men," *Esquire*; "Women," *Good Housekeeping*; "News," *Time*; "Hunting and Fishing," *Field and Stream*; "Health," *Prevention*; "Automotive," *Popular Mechanics*; "Business," *Fortune*; and "Home," *Better Homes and Gardens* (Ursic et al., 1986, p. 131).

The coders for the Ursic et al. (1986) study, one male and one female in their 60s, were asked to view each advertisement that contained an older person, identifying them by their personal appearance (i.e., gray hair, balding, posture, etc.) and the copy in the advertisement. When an advertisement with an older individual was found the coders classified the advertisement by theme (i.e., "recreational," "social," "family," "white collar," "blue collar," "miscellaneous," or "no theme"). The older model's gender and the type of product that was being advertised were also noted.

The results of the Ursic et al. (1986) study show that older individuals were shown in just 9% of the total advertisements. Between the years of 1950 and 1980 there was an increase of only 3.2% in older individuals' representation in advertisements providing no statistical significance in their numbers throughout the years. Over half (53.5%) of the older characters were shown in working situations, primarily in prestigious jobs. Product class results indicate that older people were used mostly for high-priced goods (i.e., cars, banks, cameras, etc.) providing some indication that advertisers realize the buying power of this market segment. Results of gender show that the majority of older models are male with the male appearing nines times more than the female. Older males were consistently shown in work situations while older females were used in more social and family settings.

Ursic et al. (1986) provided evidence of the under representation of the older individual in magazine advertisement throughout the 30-year study period. The selection of magazines provided periodicals with large readerships in a variety of categories, limiting those that may have been too specific or those with low adult and senior readership. The older female has consistently been ignored in advertising and this study shows what little attention they receive from magazine advertisers. A special point was made by mentioning that the coders were one female and one male both over the age of 60, yet the authors gave no reasoning for their selection or indication of how the results may have been effected by using these coders. Also, no attempt was made to distinguish between targeted and nontargeted advertisements for the older market and this information, over the test period of the past 30 years, would have been helpful.

The results of the Ursic et al. (1986) study supports the argument that if the older population is not the target market then advertisers do not worry if they are not represented in the advertisements. The findings did indicate that older models are used for higher priced items, (e.g., cars, cameras, etc.) which shows that marketers do target older consumers. The study also did not look at the role, portrayal, or personality of the older individuals only the type of theme in the advertisement. The omission of these two areas of research provides strong support for the present studies' work in targeting and role portrayal of the older individual.

In a more recent study, Peterson (1992) conducted a content analysis to determine if stereotypical representation of older individuals has changed in the past decade. His content analysis used a sample of advertisements appearing in "1989 issues of 13 national magazines widely read by individuals in all adult age groups: (1) *Reader's Digest*, 2) *Newsweek*, 3) *Business Week*, 4) *Esquire*, 5) *Gentlemen's Quarterly*, 6) *T.V. Guide*, 7) *Good Housekeeping*, 8) *Family Circle*, 9) *Woman's Day*, 10) *Time*, 11) *The New Yorker*, 12) *McCall's*, and 13) *Field and Stream*" (Peterson, 1992, p. 702). A total of 375 advertisements were designated as being designed for a specific market segment, age group, or had a certain "desirable" or "undesirable" appeal (Peterson, 1992, pp. 701-706). Coders were given 60 randomly selected advertisements and asked to determine if the advertisement was designed for consumers under 45 years old, between 45 and 64 years old, or 65 years or older. Additionally, the coders were asked to evaluate if the models in the advertisement were portrayed in a "favorable (mental and physical competence), or unfavorable (mental or physical incompetence)" way (pp. 701-706).

Peterson's (1992) results show that the majority of advertisements studied (82%) contained individuals less than 45 years of age. When the product was directed toward older people, 79% of the advertisements (*n*=99) contained models over 45. This finding is in direct contradiction to the overall results indicating that advertisers are beginning to recognize the older market. The results also indicate that models 45 years of age or older are also portrayed less favorably than the younger models. Even when the product is aimed toward an older audience, the older characters are portrayed in a somewhat undesirable manner. The largest difference in desirability and undesirability of the aged is seen in advertisements aimed at a younger audience. Although there were not a large number of advertisements with older individuals (*n*= 7), 71% were portrayed in an undesirable manner. The author believes this finding is a reinforcement of the stereotype society has placed on the aged but more importantly this depiction may reinforce the image seniors have of themselves (Peterson, 1992).

Twelve years after Gantz, Gartenberg, and Rainbow's (1980) study, Peterson's (1992) study provided similar results. According to Peterson, older individuals are underrepresented, they are portrayed in a less favorable manner, and many older characters were seen in stereotypical roles (e.g., feeble, cranky, sick). The author did examine advertisements that were targeting an older audience and found that even when they are targeted they are show negatively. The advertisements targeted at the older market did, however, have more older actors, which may indicate that marketers are recognizing the need to represent and target the older consumer.

OLDER INDIVIDUALS ON TELEVISION ADVERTISEMENTS

In addition to magazines, researchers have examined the portrayal of older individuals on television commercials. Hiemstra, Goodman, Middlemiss, Vosco, and Ziegler (1983) conducted a content analysis of a variety of half-hour time slots on weekends, weekdays, and evenings from the three major commercial networks (i.e., 1) ABC, 2) CBS, and 3) NBC) to determine the image of aging on television advertisements. The researchers examined a total of 136 commercials identifying all characters over the age of 50 but concentrating specifically on actors age 60 and over. In addition to age and other demographic data, coders identified the older individuals' appearance, behaviors, and types of roles they portrayed. The authors were interested in determining "1) the extent to which older people (50 years of age or older) are represented in television commercials, 2) the extent of the portrayal of older women, 3) the realism of the portrayal of older people, 4) how families are portrayed in relationship to older people being present, 5) the nature of the product when older people are present, and 6) the overall tone of commercials relative to any glorification of youth" (pp. 115-116).

The results of Hiemstra et al. (1983) content analysis provided information relative to the six areas of interest. First, only 32 commercials had one or more characters 50 years or older and only 11 (3.1%) commercials contained characters believed to be over the age of 60 providing little representation of the over 50 crowd. Second, the representation of women over the age of 60 was less than 1% of the total number of characters. The third area of examination was how realistic older people are portrayed in commercials. The researchers found that there was an absence of older physical characteristics such as balding men, and individuals with wrinkled skin. Hiemstra et al. (1983) explain that this is the result of advertisers portraying the old as a "young-old" with a noticeable absence of very old people (p. 117). Additionally, there was only one character from a minority group, a 50-year-old African American male. There were no minority characters found over the age of 60, which directly contradicts the census results of the time (1982) which states "that 7% of all individuals in the United States who are age 60 and older are African American" (p. 117).

Older individuals were depicted in terms of their family relationships as being alone with no observable family. Because many older individuals are involved, in some way, with a family, Hiemstra et al. (1983) found the fact that there were no grandparent roles surprising. Fifth, the advertised products with older people tended to deal with health products, food, consumer services, and household products. The age of characters was noticeably higher when a health-related product was advertised. The sixth area of interest pertained to the overall tone of the commercial in relation to youth and being young. In the commercials observed, the central character was a healthy, often sexy or macho person in his or her early thirties. Sixty-six percent of all characters were classified as under 40.

The results of Hiemstra et al. 's (1983) content analysis are much the same as those found in magazine advertisement studies. Older individuals are under represented and older females are shown less than older males. The authors did identify problems in the representation of minorities by finding only one older minority character and the lack of a family situation for the older individuals. No attempt was made to examine advertisements targeted at the older market nor did the authors identify the older characters' roles or portrayals. These areas need to be considered to better understand how older individuals are represented in advertisements.

In another study, Moore and Cadeau (1985) examined the representation of women, minorities, and older individuals on Canadian television advertisements. Their sample of advertisements was taken from Toronto-based television stations during the prime-time hours across the days of the week. Coders were instructed to gather the following information from each commercial: "1) gender of voice-overs, 2) characters roles, 3) product type, 4) setting of the advertisement, 5) all older characters, and 6) visible minorities" (Moore & Cadeau, 1985, p. 217).

The results of the Moore and Cadeau (1985) study revealed that the majority of voice-overs (88.5%) and main characters (57%) were male. The largest percentage of female main characters (41%) were shown in home settings as compared to only 7% of the male characters shown at home. Older characters were shown in 8.19% of the advertisements and minorities were in a mere 3.63% of all commercials. Older people were used most often in food commercials and least often in beauty and hygiene products. Moore and Cadeau (1985) explain that the results in each of these categories are extremely low in comparison to Canada's total population.

Moore and Cadeau's (1985) study, which concentrated mainly on the role of women in Canadian television commercials, provides results about older individuals similar to studies conducted in the United States. In Canadian television commercials, older individuals are also underrepresented in comparison to their overall population. The authors examined the use of minorities in commercials and found that their representation was even less than the older individuals. There was no information given on the use of older minorities in advertisements, which may have provided interesting results about their representation.

In a more recent study, Swayne and Greco (1987) conducted a content analysis of television commercials to determine how older individuals were represented and what roles they portrayed in the advertisements. Their study consisted of 36 hours from a variety of times periods on the three major television networks (i.e., 1) ABC, 2) CBS, 3) NBC) during the month of November. A total of 814 advertisements were viewed. The information gathered from the advertisements included "1) the number of people in the advertisements, 2) number of older people, 3) role of the older individuals (major, minor, or background), 4) type of character played by the older person (advisor, information receiver, humorous, or feeble), 5) positioning of older individuals with other people, 6) the setting of the advertisement, and 7) the intended audience" (p. 48). Older individuals in this study were defined as people 65 years or older.

The results from the Swayne and Greco (1987) study determined that older individuals were underrepresented in television advertisements (total advertisements with nonolder people was 665 while total advertisements with older people was 50). The total number of people in the television advertisements was 3,109 and only 3.2% of those individuals were over the age of 65. Older females were more frequent than older males (57 females and 43 males) and 52.6% of these advertisements contained females only.

In examining the roles of older individuals, Swayne and Greco (1987) found that in the advertisements containing older people, 56% played minor roles, 31.6% played major roles, and 12.3% played background roles. The type of characters portrayed by the majority of the older individuals was an advisor (65.2%); 15.2% were information receivers, 12% were in humorous or comical roles, and 6.5% were shown as feeble or confused. Positioning of older individuals in the advertisement have them 75% of the time appearing with people of other ages, 14% alone, 8% were all older people, and 4% were with children. The most popular setting for advertisements with older individuals was 1) the home (56%), followed by 2) business (18%), and 3) outdoors (12%).

The final area Swayne and Greco (1987) looked at was the type of products older individuals advertise. Thirty-six percent of the advertisements containing older characters were for food products with a broad appeal such as coffee, soup, and oatmeal. The next largest percentage was for public service announcements (16%) followed by retail advertising (12%), cosmetics (8%), weight control products (6%), health products (6%), and security items (4%).

Swayne and Greco's (1987) study provides valuable insight into the use of older individuals in television advertising. Their results are similar to those found in magazine and television content studies which indicates that older individuals are underrepresented in advertising and are normally used in minor roles. The researchers found that there were more women in the television advertisements, which may be due to the examination of afternoon programming. Overall, this study was excellent in determining the portrayal of older individuals in television advertising. They did not, however, examine the physical, mental, and personality traits (except for the traits of sick and feeble) which would have been helpful in understanding how the older characters are presented in television advertisements.

In a study conducted eight years after the Swayne and Greco (1987) study, Robinson, Duet, and Smith (1995) examined the portrayal of older individuals in prime-time television advertisements. The authors' intention was to replicate the Swayne and Greco study with some modification to determine if the findings were still representative. Robinson et al. looked at only prime time (7:00 p.m. to 10:00 p.m.) network television advertisements because most of the older market's television viewing is in the evening and the commercials during these hours are seen as being useful in decision making (Burnett, 1991; Schreiber & Boyd, 1980). With this information, the researchers intended to find 1) the proportion of older individuals in comparison to the total number of people in the advertisements, 2) the roles the older characters have in advertisements, 3) the type of characters portrayed by older individuals, 4) there number of people in the advertisements with older people, 5) if the older individuals are cast in stereotypical roles, and 6) if older individuals are in advertisements targeted for the older market.

Robinson et al. 's (1995) data were gathered from 36 hours of television programming on the four major networks (i.e., 1) ABC, 2) CBS, 3) FOX, 4) NBC). Coders were asked to identify all advertisements with characters over the age of 65. Subjective criteria such as wrinkles around eyes and on hands, excessive gray hair, use of an aid (cane, wheelchair, or walker), parent of a middle-aged child, a grandparent, or a reference to retirement.

Robinson et al. (1995) used a total of 714 advertisements with people as the basis for their results. Of the 1,783 people counted in the advertisements, 210 (11.8%) were older people. The number of advertisements with older men was larger than the number of advertisements with women only or with both men and women. Older men were used predominantly in major roles while older women were most often in background roles. The authors believe this is due to advertisers' relying on the older male advisor as the person best suited to sell products. As a group, older individuals were seen most often as part of the background or as a "set decoration" (p. 7). Because of their use in the background older characters did not actively participate in the advertisements and were cast mostly as neutral characters (33.4%).

Advisor roles were next (30.0%) but a limited number of comical/humorous (13.4%) or feeble/confused (4.3%) were found.

Robinson et al. (1995) found that older characters were usually placed in advertisements with multiple age groups (88.9%) instead of with children (7.1%), alone (2.4%), or with only older people (1.9%). This may be due to advertisers' using the "transgenerational approach" (French & Fox, 1985, p. 62), which states that if different age groups are used in advertisements, the advertisement will appeal to many different ages. One of the most positive findings was that outdoor settings were the most common setting for older characters which differs from past studies (Swayne & Greco, 1987). There were a wide variety of products advertised by older characters. Fast food, food products, and retail business were the most common. Of the 120 advertisements with older people, not one was directed specifically toward the older market.

The Robinson et al. (1995) study provides support that older individuals are still underrepresented in advertising and there continues to be a need for major roles for this growing market segment. The researchers did find that 93% of the older characters were shown in a positive manner, which affirms that advertisers are limiting the stereotypical images of aging. The use of prime-time advertising in this study provides excellent results for this time period; however, extending the study into other time periods may be helpful in understanding the overall portrayal of age in television advertising. The authors did examine the targeting of the older market finding that no products were targeted to this group. Extending the targeting to the other time periods and the different types of media should provide a better understanding of the amount of attention marketers are giving the older market.

A clear definition of an older person was not provided in any of the research on older individuals. The age was set at different levels (anywhere from 45 to 64 years of age) depending on the researchers. A definition of what constitutes a person being considered "old" is needed to accurately conduct and compare research in this area. Additionally, no researcher has attempted to determine the age of the older actors in television programming or magazine and television advertising. The present research will do both of these to provide a better understanding of who the older individuals are and how they are portrayed in the media.

OLDER INDIVIDUALS' RESPONSE TO ADVERTISING

With the information available about the portrayal of older individuals and how they seem to be underrepresented and portrayed in a stereotypical or negative manner (e.g., "sick," "feeble," "cranky"), determining their perception of advertising and their portrayal in advertisements would be the next logical area of discussion. Schreiber and Boyd (1980) sought to determine if older individuals find television commercials helpful in making their consumer decisions and what other factors affect their perception of television.

A self-administered questionnaire with questions about media habits and perception of advertising was distributed to a sample of 442 senior. Ninety-nine percent of the respondents indicated that they watch some television and 89% watch every day. Most older individuals preferred to watch television during the evening, 53% indicated that they watch television during the afternoon (between 2-6 p.m.), and few watched during the morning hours. The results also indicated that most commercials are seen in a positive light and the majority (69%) of the respondents said they believed commercials were useful to them in their decision making. Commercials were as being confusing or completely useless. Newspapers were seen as the most credible source of information (43%) and television was second (37%). When asked specifically about television commercials, those during the evening news were the most useful (40%), with evening programming second (15%), and daytime serials (8%) third.

Thirty-one percent of the sample believed older individuals were not often shown in advertisements. When they were shown, 57% said they thought older individuals were shown as either "active or healthy" or "likable" (p. 64). When asked about their perceptions concerning the actors in television commercials, 49% said that they "were just like the people I meet every day," and 32% said that commercials show individuals the "way I wish they would be" (p. 64). The heavy viewers were more likely to say television commercials were "realistic" while light viewers were more likely to say they were the way "I wish people were like" (p. 64).

The information found by Schreiber and Boyd (1980) was positive in relation to advertising and the way older individuals believe they are portrayed; however, other studies are not so favorable. In a study designed to determine older individuals' response to their portrayal in advertising, Festervand and Lumpkin (1985) administered a questionnaire to 271 senior citizens attending a senior citizens activity center. Their results indicated that 67% of the respondents did not enjoy television commercials. Fifty-one percent of the older sample did not believe advertisements show older people as they really are, 55% claimed that advertisements did not accurately portray the older population, and 49% believed they were portrayed as inactive and unproductive in advertisements. Seventy percent of the respondents said older individuals appeared mostly in health or medical-related advertisements and 58% believe that older people are portrayed as lonely. Overall, older individuals believed their portrayal in advertising was negative and not representative of their real lives.

In addition, Festervand and Lumpkin (1985) found that 58% of the respondents correlated the advertisement with the company and over 51% said if a product they used developed an advertising campaign that portrayed older individuals negatively, then they would stop using the product. These results show that, overall, older consumers have a negative attitudes toward advertising which may be due, as Festervand and Lumpkin (1985) state, "to a lack of credibility and an inaccurate portrayal of older individuals in advertising" (p. 220). If advertisers continue to portray the older consumer inaccurately, the effect may well be the loss of this strong segment of the economic market.

The Festervand and Lumpkin (1985) and Schreiber and Boyd (1980) studies have different responses to the way older individuals believe they are represented by advertisers. Additional studies need to be conducted to understand more clearly older individuals' perception of advertising, their portrayal in advertising, and the perception they have of themselves. Advertisers should be interested in this data because it sheds some light on their role in attracting the older market.

CHAPTER III

Methodology

To better understand the portrayal of older individuals in targeted and nontargeted advertisements, this research used a content analysis of national and local advertisements on television, and in magazines and newspapers. Because examining the portrayal of older individuals in the advertisements is the main intent of this study, all advertisements depicting people were analyzed. Advertisements containing no people, animated/computer-generated characters, network or station promotional spots, publication advertisements or "house" advertisements were not counted. Partial body parts such as hands, legs or feet were not counted as a person or character; however, close-up shots of faces were included.

There was no attempt to control for duplication of advertisements as many advertisers utilize high frequency of repetition as a technique to achieve brand recognition (Swayne & Greco, 1980). The independent coders were allowed to view the advertisements a number of times to insure accuracy on the numbers of individuals and types of roles portrayed. This researcher trained each of the independent coders on how to use the content analysis instrument; how to identify older individuals, their roles, character portrayals, physical, mental, and personality traits; and how to recognize possible problems in judgment that might occur during the coding process. Because the information in this research was designed to help determine how people in the 18-49 age group view older individuals in targeted and nontargeted advertisements, the independent coders were from the 18-49 age group.

In an attempt to minimize any coder bias that may have existed in the findings, the data from each of the coders were compared to create one set of results that was representative of each of the coders. Any questions or discrepancies that arose during the process were discussed by the coders and corrected. When a disagreement did arise, the coders were allowed to view the advertisement in question again so a decision could be made.

EXPLAINING THE CODING INSTRUMENT

The information used to construct the coding instrument was taken from similar content analysis studies whose instruments were found to be valid and reliable (Swayne & Greco, 1987; Robinson et al., 1995; Ursic et al., 1986). Each of the three media utilized the same coding instrument so that similar information could be gathered. The coding instrument was pretested by five graduate students (four males and one female in the 18 to 49 age group) at the University of Southern Mississippi for ease of reading and ability to gather the desired information.

The instrument was divided into three sections. The first section identified the specific television network, magazine, or newspaper, specific information about the media source (i.e., network time, publication size, and date), and the brand and product category in the specific advertisement. The second section is where coders tabulated the number of people, number of older people, and the number of older males and females appearing in the advertisement. Section three was used to record specific information about the portrayal of the older individual(s) in the advertisements which includes the older character's approximate age, celebrity status, their role, the character they played, their mental, physical, and personality traits, and the setting of the advertisement. In addition, the coders were asked to determine the specific age demographic each advertisement was targeted toward, and whether the overall portrayal of the older character(s) was positive or negative.

Coders were instructed to identify all older characters using subjective criteria such as 1) an appearance of retirement, 2) extensive gray hair, 3) wrinkles of the skin around the eyes and/or hands, 4) use of aids such as canes or wheelchairs, 5) the parent of a son or daughter who is middle-aged or older, or 6) evidence of grandchildren or great-grandchildren (Gantz et al. 1980; Peterson, 1992; Swayne & Greco, 1987). Only people whose faces were shown and could be identified by age and gender were counted. For example, a person sitting in the background at a distance where his or her face was not clearly exposed was not counted. In addition to the stated categories, coders were given characteristic profiles of older individuals, the different roles, character portrayals, mental, physical and personality traits, and settings to ensure accuracy in the data reporting.

The specific techniques for gathering the information in the content analysis for each of the three types of media are as follows:

MAGAZINES

The advertisements appearing in a sample of 1994-95 issues of 10 general interest magazines were used for the content analysis. The magazines were selected because, according to *Simmons 1994 Study of Media and Markets*, they are widely read by individuals in all adult age group demographic categories (18-34, 18-49, 35-54, and 55-64) including the older demographic (65 and older) (p. Q373). Publications that appeal to specific age groups, such as *Modern Maturity* and *Seventeen,* were avoided so the results would not be biased either with or without a large number of older people. Four randomly selected issues (1 from each quarter of the year) from each of the 10 magazines were selected for a total of 40 magazines. The magazines were then viewed and coded by the independent coders.

NEWSPAPERS

A sample of advertisements appearing in the 1995 issues of selected newspapers was utilized for the content analysis. A total of eight newspapers were selected representing papers with 1) a large circulation (over 1 million), 2) a medium circulation (100,000 to 500,00), and 3) a small circulation (25,000 to 50,000) (Standard Rate and Data Service, Daily Newspaper Edition, 1984). One issue from each paper was selected from six different months in 1995 for a total of 48 newspapers. These six issues provided a representation of three-quarters of the year. The newspapers were then viewed and coded by the independent coders who were instructed to code only the advertisements included as part of the newspapers. No inserts, coupons, or newspaper magazines (e.g., *USA Today Weekend, Parade*) were coded as part of this study.

TELEVISION

The advertisements were videotaped from each of the four major commercial networks (i.e., 1) ABC, 2) CBS, 3) FOX and 4) NBC) on two days during the week (one weekday and one day of the weekend). Three different time slots were taped in an attempt to cover all types of programming, times, and audience demographics. The times that were examined were based on the *Simmons* criteria for evaluating television programming: 1) midday (11:00 a.m. to 3:00 p.m.), 2) late afternoon (3:00 p.m. to 7:00 p.m.), and 3) prime time (7:00 p.m. to 10:00 p.m.) (Simmons, 1994). Eleven hours were taped each day on each of the four networks for a total of 88 hours of programming. The videotapes were then watched and coded by the independent coders.

CHAPTER IV

Analysis of Data

INTRODUCTION

The three independent coders evaluated 40 magazines with a total of 1,130 advertisements, 48 newspapers with a total of 1,081 advertisements, and 88 hours of television with a total of 1,770 advertisements.

Information in the intercoder reliability is found in Table 1. Descriptive information about the number of advertisements, the number of people in the advertisements, and the number of older males and females are reported in Tables 2-4. Table 5 addresses the number of advertisements targeted at the different age demographic groups.

Information about the portrayal of the older characters in the advertisements is reported in Tables 6-11. Data on the products advertised, types of roles, the character type, mental, physical, or personality characteristics, setting of the advertisement, positioning of the older character with others, and the overall portrayal is included in these tables.

RESULTS OF THE CODING INSTRUMENT PRETEST

The original coding instrument was pretested by five graduate students for ease of reading and ability to gather the desired information. Recommendations were made on improving the construction and text of the instrument. The suggested changes for the content included 1) adding the section on age so the coders could estimate the age of the older individuals and 2) increasing the number of choices in the portrayal section of the instrument (e.g., cast as, types of person, setting).

The changes were made and the final coding instrument was completed. Overall the pretest proved helpful in creating a coding instrument that was effective in gathering the desired information for this study.

RESULTS OF INTERCODER RELIABILITY

To eliminate the possibility of coder bias, the findings from each of the independent coders were compared to determine a percentage of agreement. In order to determine the intercoder reliability in terms of agreement, Holsti's (1969) reliability formula was used (as cited in Wimmer & Dominick, 1991). The percentages of agreement between the coders for each of the different media are provided in Table 1.

Table 1: Independent Coder Reliability of Content Analysis

Media sources	Percentage of agreement
Magazines	98.0%
Newspapers	87.0%
Television	96.0%

For the advertisements where there was not an agreement, the discrepancies or questions were discussed and corrected. If necessary, the coders were allowed to view the advertisements a second time in order to come to an agreement. According to Kassarjian (1977), agreement coefficients above 85% are satisfactory in a content analysis study. The percentages of agreements between coders in this content analysis are well within the acceptable range.

RESULTS OF THE RESEARCH QUESTIONS

The following results are presented in order of the research questions. The first research question examined the representation of the older population in magazines, in newspapers advertisements, and on television advertisements.

RQ1: Is the number of older individuals appearing in selected advertisements in the media less than their actual number of the population?

The total number of advertisements coded in the content analysis from all three of the media (i.e., 1) magazines, 2) newspapers, and 3) television) was 3,990 and the total number of people in the advertisements was 12,818. Table 2 shows the total number of advertisements and the total number of advertisements containing at least one older (age 65 and older) person (the total number of advertisements and advertisements with older individuals in each of the magazines and newspapers and on each of the television networks is shown in Appendix A).

Table 2: Total Number of Advertisements with People and Older Individuals in the Media

Media sources	Total number of ads (N)	Total number of ads with older people (n)	Percentage of older people in ads
Magazines	1,139	102	9.0%
Newspapers	1,081	89	8.2%
Television	1,770	284	16.1%
TOTAL (N)	3,990	475	12.0%

The number of advertisements containing an older person is high in magazines (9.0%) and newspapers (8.2%) but still less than the actual percentage of older peoples in the United States. According to the United States Bureau of the Census the number of older Americans is 13% of the total United States Population (Schick, 1986). Sixteen percent of the advertisements on television had at least one older person, well above the national percentage (13%) of older people and more than both magazines (9.0%) and newspapers (8.2%). The 16.1% of advertisements on television was the same percentage Robinson et al. (1995) found. They discovered that 16.8% of the advertisements on prime-time television had at least one older person. In an earlier study, Swayne and Greco (1987) determined that 6.9% of the advertisements, in a variety of time slots, contained at least one older person. The results of this research verify that over the past 10 years the total number of television advertisements with an older character has increased.

Past content analyses on the representation of older individuals in magazine advertisements have discovered the percentages of older characters to be small in comparison to other age groups. Gantz et al. (1980) found that older characters where represented in 5.9% of the advertisements and Peterson (1992) found in his content analysis of general interest magazines that older individuals were in 5.0% of the advertisements. In a longitudinal study of general interest magazine advertisements, Ursic et al. (1986) found that older individuals were in 9.0% of the advertisements over the past 30 years. The present study's findings that 9.0% of the advertisements have an older character support what Ursic et al. (1986) found and proves that the number of older individuals in magazine advertisements has remained the same since the 1950s. Having an older person in only 8.2% of the advertisements is a low percentage, especially when the fact that older people are the largest regular readers of newspapers is considered (Newspaper Advertising Bureau, as cited in Schick, 1986).

The present study has shown that in the general interest media the older population is well represented and they appear in a number of advertisements (12.0%) in proportion to their actual population numbers. Also, the results obtained from the advertisements in newspapers add to the past research in magazines and television needed information on the portrayal and representation of older individuals in the media.

When the total number of people and the total number of older individuals appearing in the advertisements are examined, the results are much different. Because many advertisements contained more than one person and/or more than one older person, examining the total number of people was necessary. Looking at the total number of individuals in an advertisement provides a better understanding of how each of the characters are represented and portrayed in comparison to other characters. Table 3 indicates the number of people and the number of older individuals in the three media (the total number of people and older individuals in each of the magazines and newspapers and on each of the television networks is shown in Appendix B).

Table 3: Total Number of People and Older Individuals in the Media Advertisements

Media sources	Total number of people in ads (N)	Total number of older people in ads (n)	Percentage of older people in ads
Magazines	2,302	132	5.7%
Newspapers	2,638	125	4.7%
Television	7,878	425	5.4%
TOTAL (N)	12,818	682	5.3%

As shown in Table 3, magazines have the lowest number of people (2,303) but the highest percentage of older individuals (5.7%), while newspaper advertisements had the lowest percentage of older individuals (4.7%). The presents study's findings of 5.4% older individuals on television is higher than Hiemstra et al. (1983) and Swayne and Greco's (1987) results of 10 years ago. Hiemstra et al. discovered 3.1% and Swayne and Greco found only 3.2% of all people in television advertisements were age 65 or older. Robinson et al. (1995), however, determined that 11.8% of the people in their content analysis of prime-time television were older indicating a decline over the past year. Television network programming executives have made clear the belief that their future is in younger audiences. For example, CBS, known in the past as the older people's network (Diamond & Ohringer, 1993), had 20.7% older people in the advertisements in the Robinson et al. study and only 6.5% (see Appendix B) in the present study.

The percentage of older people in magazine advertisements is also higher than in past studies. Gantz et al. (1980) found that only 3.1% of the people in advertisements were older. While the present studies' finding of 5.7% is higher than past research, the percentage is still lower than the actual percentage of the older population (13%). The total number of older individuals in all three media were only 5.4%, indicating that older individuals are underrepresented in the general interest media. Ninety-five percent of the people seen in advertisements are under the age of 65 placing the older population at a point of nonexistence in advertisements, a situation about which older individuals and advertisers should be concerned. The results from the present study support the findings from past research that the older population is underrepresented in advertising and that over the years their numbers have not improved (Gantz et al., 1980; Hiemstra et al., 1983; Robinson et al., 1995; Swayne & Greco, 1987).

When the total number of older characters are divided along gender lines, the results indicate that the majority (68.2%) are male (see Table 4). Seventy-three percent of the older characters in magazines, 72% in newspapers, and 66% on television were male. The advertisements with an older male on television were the same as the percentage found in the Robinson et al. (1995) study (66.7%). These numbers also support past studies which found that older women are seen far less than older men (Gantz et al., 1980; Harris & Feinberg, 1977; Hiemstra et al., 1983; Northcott, 1975; Smith, 1976; Ursic et al., 1986). Older females' percentage of the older character in the media (31.8%) is in direct contradiction to their real-life numbers because females live, on average, six to seven years longer than males (Schick, 1986). Advertisers' failure to adequately represent the older female population indicates, first, a lack of understanding of the older market and; second, failure to target a group with very large numbers and spending power (Linden, 1985; Schick, 1986).

In response to the first research question, older individuals are well represented in the total number of advertisements with an older person appearing in 12% of all advertisements. The older population is, however, underrepresented in their total numbers, totaling only 5.2% of all of the individuals in advertisements. In the three media studied, older females appear in advertisements far less than older males.

Table 4: Total Number of Older Individuals by Gender

Gender	Magazines n (%)	Newspapers n (%)	Television n (%)	Total media (N)
Male	96 (73.0%)	90 (72.0%)	279 (65.6%)	465 (68.0%)
Female	36 (27.0%)	35 (28.0%)	146 (34.4%)	217 (32.0%)
TOTAL (N)	132 (100%)	125 (100%)	425 (100%)	682 (100%)

The next six research questions examine the targeting of the older market in media advertisements. Only one study has considered the portrayal of older individuals in advertisements targeted at older and younger markets (Peterson, 1992). Peterson's research was limited to an overall portrayal (desirable or undesirable) of the characters in each advertisement. Other research on the portrayal of older individuals did not divide the advertisements into targeted segments. The present research was conducted to determine the amount of advertisements and the difference in the portrayal of older individuals in targeted and nontargeted advertisements. Research question two sought to determine the total number of advertisement in the media which target the older market, and the third research question looks at the type of products that are targeting the older market.

RQ2: What number of selected advertisements in the electronic and print media target older individuals?

Table 5 indicates the number of advertisements containing at least one older person targeting the specific target markets. The number of advertisements targeting the older market is high in magazines (22.5%) and newspapers (16.9%) when compared to those targeted at a younger audience (magazines, 22.5% and newspaper, 18.0%). There were 111 (39.1%) television commercials targeting the younger market and only 46 (16.2%) that targeted the older market. Television's main target audience is individuals age 18 to 49 (Castro, 1989; Seligson, 1993; Taylor, 1995) and the results confirm that even when there is an older person in the advertisement, the younger audience is targeted more often.

Table 5: Number of Advertisements Targeting the Different Market Segments

Advertisements targeted toward	Magazines n (%)	Newspapers n (%)	Television n (%)	Total media N (%)
18 to 49	23 (22.5%)	16 (18.0%)	111 (39.1%)	150 (31.6%)
Older market	23 (22.5%)	15 (16.9%)	46 (16.2%)	84 (17.7%)
All consumers	56 (55.0%)	58 (65.1%)	127 (44.7%)	241 (50.7%)
TOTAL (N)	102 (100%)	89 (100%)	284 (100%)	475 (100%)

The largest percentage of advertisements (magazines 55.0%; newspapers 65.1%; television 44.7%) with an older character were those targeting all consumers. Advertisements that had no mention of age or for a product designed for a particular age group were considered part of the "All Consumers" category. For example, Wendy's and Wal-Mart both target a wide variety of age groups while McDonald's (with Ronald McDonald) and the GAP (a clothing store) have very specific audiences. French and Fox (1985) suggest that the inclusion of all ages in an advertisement makes the product and advertisements seem more "transgenerational" (p. 62). By being transgenerational an advertisements can appeal to the general population, which includes the older market. From the present study's results, 51% of the advertisements with an older character, are created to attract "All Consumers." The latter result suggests that marketers are reluctant to associate their products with all older people and would rather try the transgenerational approach (Swayne & Greco, 1987).

This research has examined the targeting of the older market in comparison to other age demographic groups. The finding that 18% of the advertisements in the media target the older market demonstrates that marketers are looking at the aged as potential buyers. Even though the number of older targeted advertisements is smaller than those targeting the younger audience the numbers that exist are greater than the 13% of the total number of older people in the United States population. The next question that is proposed in research question three is what kinds of products do marketers and advertisers target toward the older audience?

RQ3: Are advertisements targeting older individuals related to their health (e.g., medicines, vitamins, insurance, etc.)?

Table 6 lists all of the advertised products that targeted the older Market. In some advertisements, targeting the older audience with an actor younger than 65 was used to advertise the products (in magazines 27 times, in newspapers 3 times, in television 18 times). The use of younger actors created a total of 84 advertisements targeting the older market (magazines 50, newspapers 18, and television 64). The results in Table 6 reveal that the majority of advertisements in the selected media (magazines 78.0%; newspapers 50.0%; television 67.2%) which target the older market are for health-related products. A total of 70% of the advertisements in the selected media targeting the older market were for health-related products. Products such as 1) medicines, 2) arthritis rubs, 3) denture care items, 4) vitamins, and 5) nutrition supplemental drinks were included in this category.

Other products and services related to health such as 1) life and health insurance, 2) rest homes, and 3) funeral homes were also advertised. If these numbers are included in a category of overall health-related products, the percentages are even higher (magazines, 86.0%; newspapers, 72.2%; television, 87.5%). Harris and Feinberg (1977) found in their study that the majority of advertisements with older characters on television were for health-related products. In addition to health-related products, the older market was targeted for a wide variety of goods and services (i.e., three beauty products, one food item, one mature readers' magazine, one destination, and one clothing item). Financial services were the only item, other than health products, that was advertised in all three of the selected media. The products in the "Other" category included 1) an IBM computer, 2) a music album by Andy Griffith, 3) a law firm specializing in helping older individuals receive their social security checks, 4) an electric company, 5) two children's board games, and 6) an anti-drug public service announcement.

Other researchers who have studied the portrayal of older individuals in the media have not looked at products specifically targeted at the older market but have determined the type of advertised products in which an older person appears. Robinson et al. (1995)

Portraying Older People in Advertising

Table 6: Advertised Products Targeting the Older Market

Products targeted at older market	Magazine n (%)	Newspapers n (%)	Television n (%)
Health	39 (78.0%)	9 (50.0%)	43 (67.2%)
Insurance	4 (8.0%)	0 (0.0%)	9 (14.1%)
Financial	2 (4.0%)	2 (11.0%)	1 (1.6%)
Rest home	0 (0.0%)	4 (22.2%)	0 (0.0%)
Funeral home	0 (0.0%)	0 (0.0%)	4 (6.2%)
Beauty	3 (6.0%)	0 (0.0%)	0 (0.0%)
Food	0 (0.0%)	0 (0.0%)	2 (3.1%)
Magazines	0 (0.0%)	1 (5.6%)	0 (0.0%)
Travel	0 (0.0%)	1 (5.6%)	0 (0.0%)
Clothing	1 (2.0%)	0 (0.0%)	0 (0.0%)
Other	1 (2.0%)	1 (5.6%)	5 (7.8%)
TOTAL (N)(%)	50 (100%)	18 (100%)	64 (100%)

found that on television advertisements, the largest number of older people were in advertisements for fast food restaurants and food products and that no older people were in advertisements for health related products. Swayne and Greco (1987) also reported that on television 36% of the older individuals in their study were in food product advertisements and 6% were in health-related advertisements. In a study of magazine advertisements, Ursic et al. (1986), reported that older character were most often in liquor advertisements (20.9%) and in 10.8% of the advertisements for health and medicine products. One set of researchers did observe that the majority of advertisements with an older person were for health-related products (Harris & Feinberg, 1977).

The past research in this area does indicate that older characters are used in advertisements for a variety of different products including those for health related products. When the advertisements that target the older market in the media are examined, however, the results clearly show that the majority (70%) are for health products. To illustrate the point further, out of the 132 advertisements that were targeted specifically toward the older market, 92 were for health products, 13 for life and health insurance, 4 for rest homes, and 4 for funeral homes, leaving only 19 for other types of products. Because there were advertisements in the study that contained more than one older person, the remainder of the results will be described using the total number of people and the total number of older people in the advertisements (see Table 3). Additionally, the total number of older people in advertisements targeting the older market and the younger audience will be used to report the results (see Table 5). There were a total of 159 older people in advertisements targeting the older market (magazines, 41; newspapers, 26; television, 92). Research question four seeks to determine how each the older characters are portrayed in advertisements in which they were the target market. The older people's roles, character casting, portrayal, and placement with others, Tables 7-10 are used to answer research question four.

RQ4: Do advertisements targeting the older market portray the older characters in a positive manner?

The first area in the portrayal of older individuals in advertisements targeting the older demographic is the type of roles they were given. Table 7 provides a listing of the major roles (dominant character), minor roles (secondary character), and background roles (only used as a background setting) for each of the older characters. The center column on Table 7 lists the older characters that appeared in advertisements targeted at the older market. Sixty-two percent of older character roles in the advertisements targeting the older market were major roles. All of the older characters in magazines (100%), and 61.5% in newspapers had major roles, proving that when the older market is the target, advertisers are placing older characters in the advertisements and giving them the major parts. Some minor roles were depicted in newspapers (38.5%) and on television (28.3). Television was the only medium, however, where the majority of roles were not major. On television, 28.3% of the roles were minor and 27.0% were background roles, which indicates that on television, even when the older market is the target, older characters do not have the dominant roles. Television executives and advertisers' lack of confidence in the older market may be the reason younger actors receive the major roles while older actors are placed in minor and background positions.

The present study has shown that in all three media, when the older market is the target for the product, older actors are being featured as the main characters in the advertisements. Advertisers are realizing that using older characters in advertisements designed to attract the business of the older consumer is an effective way to sell their products.

The type of characters the older people were cast as in the advertisements is the next area in the portrayal of older individuals (see Table 8). The center column of Table 8 lists the older characters appearing in advertisements targeted at the older market. The largest percentage of characters in all three media (1) magazines, 75.6%; 2) newspapers, 23.1%; 3) television, 12.0%) were cast as either a husband or a wife. Harris and Feinberg (1977) found that the majority of older people on television programs (e.g., dramas, game shows, situation comedies, etc.) were shown in a married situation. Advertisers are now using this acceptable, comfortable role to sell products to the older market.

The "Other/None" category included older characters that were not cast in a particular role or they were used in a role that could not be placed in one of the existing categories (e.g., entertainer, student, and model). In newspaper and magazine advertisements, a number of photographs or pictures of a model's face were included in the Other/None category. On television there was a large number of older spokespersons (e.g., Ed McMahan and Dick Clark for the Publisher's Clearing House Sweepstakes), models (e.g., pictured wearing the advertised clothing), and entertainers promoting their films, television programs and plays (e.g., Gene Hackman, Morgan Freeman).

Two areas with low overall percentages were "Parent" (magazines, 2.4%; newspapers, 0.0%; television, 4.3%) and "Grandparent" (magazines, 7.3%; newspapers, 3.8%; television, 4.3%) which is surprising because older people are often found in one or both of these roles. The casting for the older characters in advertisements targeted at the older market was very positive with a high percentage of husband and wife roles. The type of role casting in advertisements has never been studied in the portrayal of older individuals. The casting criterion adds to this research by describing the types of characters the older individuals are cast as and helps to clarify their overall portrayal in media advertisements

Table 7: The Older Characters' Roles in the Advertisements

MAGAZINES

Role	Ads targeted toward under 49 n (%)	Ads targeted toward older market n (%)	Ads targeted toward all consumers n (%)
Major	7 (31.8%)	41 (100%)	45 (65.2%)
Minor	15 (68.2%)	0 (0.0%)	24 (34.8%)
TOTAL (N)(%)	22 (100%)	41 (100%)	69 (100%)

NEWSPAPERS

Role	Ads targeted toward under 49 n (%)	Ads targeted toward older market n (%)	Ads targeted toward all consumers n (%)
Major	5 (27.8%)	16 (61.5%)	28 (34.6%)
Minor	13 (72.2%)	10 (38.5%)	52 (64.2%)
Background	0 (0.0%)	0 (0.0%)	1 (1.2%)
TOTAL (N)(%)	18 (100%)	26 (100%)	81 (100%)

TELEVISION

Role	Ads targeted toward under 49 n (%)	Ads targeted toward older market n (%)	Ads targeted toward all consumers n (%)
Major	33 (24.8%)	41 (44.5%)	75 (37.5%)
Minor	68 (51.1%)	26 (28.3%)	78 (39.0%)
Background	32 (24.1%)	25 (27.2%)	47 (23.5%)
TOTAL (N)(%)	133 (100%)	92 (100%)	200 (100%)

Table 8: Type of Person the Older Person Was Cast as in the Advertisements

Older person cast in magazines as	Ads targeted at under 49	Ads targeted at older market	Ads targeted at all consumers
Consumer	1 (4.5%)	1 (2.4%)	16 (23.2%)
Husband/Wife	0 (0.0%)	31 (75.6%)	4 (5.8%)
Grandparent	2 (9.1%)	3 (7.3%)	5 (7.2%)
Parent	0 (0.0%)	1 (2.4%)	1 (1.4%)
Owner/Boss	1 (4.5%)	0 (0.0%)	12 (17.4%)
Worker	2 (9.1%)	2 (4.9%)	3 (4.3%)
Other/None	16 (72.7%)	3 (7.3%)	28 (40.5%)
TOTAL (N)(%)	22 (100%)	41 (100%)	69 (100%)

NEWSPAPERS

Older person cast in newspapers as	Ads targeted at under 49	Ads targeted at older market	Ads targeted at all consumers
Consumer	0 (0.0%)	6 (23.1%)	2 (2.5%)
Husband/Wife	0 (0.0%)	6 (23.1%)	6 (7.4%)
Grandparent	0 (0.0%)	1 (3.8%)	0 (0.0%)
Parent	0 (0.0%)	0 (0.0%)	0 (0.0%)
Owner/Boss	0 (0.0%)	2 (7.7%)	9 (11.1%)
Worker	3 (16.7%)	3 (11.5%)	7 (8.6%)
Other/None	15 (83.4%)	8 (30.8%)	57 (70.4%)
TOTAL (N)(%)	18 (100%)	26 (100%)	81 (100%)

TELEVISION

Older person cast on television as	Ads targeted at under 49	Ads targeted at older market	Ads targeted at all consumers
Consumer	6 (4.5%)	4 (4.3%)	17 (8.5%)
Husband/Wife	12 (9.0%)	11 (12.0%)	10 (5.0%)
Grandparent	15 (11.4%)	4 (4.3%)	33 (16.5%)
Parent	5 (3.8%)	4 (4.3%)	4 (2.0%)
Owner/Boss	22 (16.5%)	7 (7.6%)	36 (18.0%)
Worker	22 (16.5%)	3 (3.3%)	13 (6.5)
Other/None	51 (38.3%)	59 (64.1%)	87 (43.5%)
TOTAL (N)(%)	133 (100%)	92 (100%)	200 (100%)

Next, the results of the older persons' mental, physical, or personality traits seen in the advertisements are presented in Table 9. The center column in Table 9 lists the portrayals in advertisements targeted toward the older market. The largest percentages in each of the three media are 1) "Happy/Content" (magazines, 58.5%; newspapers,

Table 9: Physical, Mental, or Personality Traits of the Older Characters

MAGAZINES

Older person portrayed in magazines as	Ads targeted toward under 49 n (%)	Ads targeted toward older market n (%)	Ads targeted toward all consumers n (%)
Angry/Disgruntled	2 (9.1%)	0 (0.0%)	1 (1.4%)
Active/Healthy	1 (4.5%)	14 (34.1%)	1 (1.4%)
Competent/Intelligent	3 (13.6%)	0 (0.0%)	7 (10.1%)
Happy/Content	7 (31.8%)	24 (58.5%)	32 (46.4%)
Humorous/Comical	3 (13.6%)	0 (0.0%)	13 (18.8%)
Sexy/Macho	0 (0.0%)	0 (0.0%)	1 (1.4%)
Sick/Feeble	2 (9.1%)	2 (4.9%)	1 (1.4%)
Other/None	4 (18.2%)	1 (2.4%)	13 (18.8%)
TOTAL (N)(%)	22 (100%)	41 (100%)	69 (100%)

NEWSPAPERS

Older person portrayed in newspapers as	Ads targeted toward under 49 n (%)	Ads targeted toward older market n (%)	Ads targeted toward all consumers n (%)
Angry/Disgruntled	0 (0.0%)	0 (0.0%)	2 (2.5%)
Active/Healthy	0 (0.0%)	4 (15.4%)	3 (3.7%)
Competent/Intelligent	0 (0.0%)	0 (0.0%)	22 (27.2%)
Happy/Content	6 (33.3%)	18 (69.2%)	27 (33.3%)
Humorous/Comical	1 (5.6%)	0 (0.0%)	6 (7.4%)
Sexy/Macho	0 (0.0%)	0 (0.0%)	1 (1.2%)
Sick/Feeble	1 (5.6%)	3 (11.5%)	2 (2.5%)
Other/None	10 (55.6%)	1 (3.8%)	18 (22.2%)
TOTAL (N)(%)	18 (100%)	26 (100%)	81 (100%)

TELEVISION

Older person portrayed on television as	Ads targeted toward under 49 n (%)	Ads targeted toward older market n (%)	Ads targeted toward all consumers n (%)
Angry/Disgruntled	13 (9.8%)	1 (1.1%)	8 (4.0%)
Active/Healthy	1 (0.7%)	15 (16.3%)	9 (4.5%)
Competent/Intelligent	9 (6.8%)	7 (7.6%)	25 (12.5%)
Happy/Content	52 (39.1%)	36 (39.1%)	130 (65.0%)
Humorous/Comical	44 (33.1%)	0 (0.0%)	8 (4.0%)
Sick/Feeble	6 (4.5%)	21 (22.8%)	7 (3.5)
Other/None	8 (6.0%)	12 (13.0%)	13 (6.5%)
TOTAL (N)(%)	133 (100%)	92 (100%)	200 (100%)

69.2%; television, 39.1%), followed by 2) "Active/Healthy" (magazines, 34.1%; newspapers, 15.4%; television, 16.3%). Schreiber and Boyd (1980) ask older individuals how they believed they were portrayed in advertisements and 57% said they thought they were portrayed as either "active and healthy" or "likable" (p. 64). The results from this study support the belief that older people, when they are the target market for the product, are shown in a desirable manner.

The one negative result that was found was the 22.8% portrayed as "Sick/Feeble" on television and the 11.5% in newspapers. The large number of health-related advertisements on television (67.2%) and in newspapers (50.0%) may be the reason why so many of the older characters were portrayed as sick or feeble. Showing a person taking the advertised medicine for an illness or rubbing on a medicated cream is a common way to advertise a health-related product (e.g., an advertisement for Ben Gay Arthritis Formula has an older woman relieving her pain by using the product). Even with the high "Sick/Feeble" percentage, the desirable traits of "Happy/Content," "Active/Healthy," and "Competent/Intelligent" were the overall majority (65%) in all three media.

Determining the physical, mental and personality characteristics of the older characters in media advertisements is new to the research in this area. Knowing the characteristics each of the older characters possesses adds to the overall understanding of the older individual's portrayal.

The final area detailing the older characters' portrayal is whom they are shown with in the advertisements (see Table 10). In advertisements targeting the older population, older characters are shown most often "Alone" (magazines, 90.2%; newspapers, 50.0%; television, 13.0%) and "With All Older People" (newspapers, 34.6%; television, 56.5%). The "Alone" category did include advertisements with a "Husband/Wife" couple, which may account for the higher number in this category, but showing a single older person or an older couple alone was common. The large percentage of advertisements with an older person positioned alone helps to explain the low total number of older people in the advertisements (see Table 3). Placing older people by themselves in advertisements, however, adds to the stereotype that all older people are alone (individually or as a couple). Television did have more advertisements (56.5%) with "All Older People" which is a positive position for older people on television. The appearance of an older person with other adults, children only or with mixed ages was infrequent in all three media.

Overall, in advertisements targeting the older market, the older characters were portrayed very positively. Peterson (1992) reported that "72% of the older individuals in magazine advertisements were

Table 10: Placement of the Older Person with Others in the Advertisements

MAGAZINES

Placement of older person(s) in ad	Ads targeted toward under 49 n (%)	Ads targeted toward older market n (%)	Ads targeted toward all consumers n (%)
Alone	7 (31.8%)	37 (90.2%)	37 (53.6%)
w/ All Older	0 (0.0%)	0 (0.0%)	6 (8.7%)
w/ Other Adults	11 (50.0%)	1 (2.4%)	19 (27.5%)
w/ Children	2 (9.1%)	3 (7.3%)	3 (4.3%)
w/ Mixed Ages	2 (9.1%)	0 (0.0%)	4 (5.9%)
TOTAL (N)(%)	22 (100%)	41 (100%)	69 (100%)

NEWSPAPERS

Placement of older person(s) in ad	Ads targeted toward under 49 n (%)	Ads targeted toward older market n (%)	Ads targeted toward all consumers n (%)
Alone	6 (33.3%)	13 (50.0%)	28 (34.6%)
w/ All Older	1 (5.6%)	9 (34.6%)	15 (18.5%)
w/ Other Adults	11 (61.1%)	3 (11.5%)	34 (42.0%)
w/ Children	0 (0.0%)	1 (3.8%)	0 (0.0%)
w/ Mixed Ages	0 (0.0%)	0 (0.0%)	4 (4.9%)
TOTAL (N)(%)	18 (100%)	26 (100%)	81 (100%)

TELEVISION

Placement of older person(s) in ad	Ads targeted toward under 49 n (%)	Ads targeted toward older market n (%)	Ads targeted toward all consumers n (%)
Alone	14 (10.5%)	12 (13.0%)	30 (15.0%)
w/ All Older	6 (4.5%)	52 (56.5%)	32 (16.0%)
w/ Other Adults	69 (51.9%)	19 (20.7%)	71 (35.5%)
w/ Children	8 (6.0%)	4 (4.3%)	6 (3.0%)
w/ Mixed Ages	36 (27.1%)	5 (5.4%)	61 (60.5%)
TOTAL (N)(%)	133 (100%)	92 (100%)	200 (100%)

portrayed in a "desirable" manner in advertisements targeting people age 45 and older" (p. 704). The present study supports the findings of Peterson, and has provided additional information on the targeting and the overall portrayal of older individuals in advertisements. The areas of the portrayals included the older characters' roles, how they were cast, how they were portrayed, and who they were positioned with in the advertisements have been examined and reported. In the present study older characters, in advertisements targeting the older market, were shown as having a "Major" role, cast as a "Husband/Wife," "Owner/Boss," or "Worker/Employee," and were portrayed as "Happy/Content" or "Active/Healthy."

In addition to understanding how older individuals are portrayed in advertisements targeted toward their own demographic, determining their portrayal in advertisements targeting a younger market will help in recognizing any stereotypes that exists. Research question five examines the percentage of older people in advertisements targeting individuals age 49 and younger. Data from Tables 7-10 is used to answer research question five.

RQ5: Do advertisements targeting the younger audience portray the older characters in a stereotypical manner?

The first column in Table 7 lists the type of roles the older character played in the advertisements targeting the younger audience. The results indicate that in all three media, the largest percentage of roles were minor (magazines, 68.2%; newspapers, 72.2%; television, 51.1%). When the younger audience is the target, older characters are only featured as major characters in 31.8% of roles in magazines and 27.8% in newspapers. On television, which also had a large number of background roles (24.1%), older characters received only 24.8% of the major roles. These numbers support the findings from Swayne and Greco (1987) who reported that 56.0% of the roles for older characters were minor. Robinson et al. (1995) also determined that the majority of background and minor roles (81.3%) went to the older characters.

The results from this study have shown that when a younger audience is the target for a product, advertisers use younger individuals in the major roles. In addition, the results show a difference in the type of roles the older characters have in the advertisement depending on who is the target market. Placing the older characters in the majority (74.0%) of minor and background roles when they are not the target market is a stereotypical position for the aged.

The types of characters older individuals are cast as are shown in the first column of Table 8. In magazines and newspapers there were no dominant roles; however, some older characters were shown as "Worker/Employee" and "Owner/Boss." On television, older characters had several different roles, but 16.5% of the characters were cast as a

"Worker/Employee" and 16.5% were cast as an "Owner/Boss." Newspapers' only identifiable role was the "Worker/Employee" (16.7%). There were more "Grandparent" portrayals (magazines, 9.1%; television 11.4%) which would include an older person as a family member in many advertisements targeted at the younger audience.

The largest percentage of roles in all three media (1) magazines, 72.7%; 2) newspapers, 83.4%; and 3) television, 38.3%) was the "Other/None" category. When only a picture of the person's face was shown or the person was not given a part in the advertisements (e.g., sitting on a park bench, walking down the road) the character was categorized as "Other/None." Additionally, an actor who was in a promotional advertisement for his or her movie, play, or television show was placed in this category. The photographs and entertainment advertisements appearing in newspapers and magazines account for the high percentages of "Other/None" in these two media.

The results provide evidence that when the data is divided by target market, the older characters are cast differently. For example, when the older market was the target the older characters were most often seen, in all three media, as a husband or a wife (30.2%). When the younger audience was the target market there were only 12 (7.0%) husband or wife roles, all on television.

The next area in the portrayal of older individuals in advertisements targeting the younger audience is the type of physical, mental and personality characteristics displayed by the older individuals (see the first column of Table 9). The characteristic of "Happy/Content" received the highest percentages in each media source (magazines, 31.8%; newspapers, 33.3%; television, 39.1%). There were only 2, "Active/Healthy" roles and 12 "Competent/Intelligent" roles in all three media. The characteristics of "Angry/Disgruntled," "Sick/Feeble," "Humorous/Comical" had low percentages in the media; however, when they are considered together as undesirable characteristics, the results show that the older characters are portrayed in this undesirable manner in a large percentage of the advertisements (magazines, 31.8%; newspapers, 11.2%; television, 47.4%). In all three media combined, 41.2% of the older characters are portrayed as having one of these undesirable characteristics.

Again the results show that when the advertisements are divided by target market the older characters are portrayed differently. In the advertisements targeting the older audience only 15.1% of the older characters were show with one of the undesirable characteristics. When the older market was the target there were zero "Humorous/Comical" portrayals and only one "Angry/Disgruntled" portrayal. In contrast, when the younger market was the target there were 48 "Humorous/Comical" portrayals and 15 "Angry/Disgruntled" portrayals. These results show that when the advertisements are not targeting the older market, the older individuals are shown in a more stereotypical manner.

The final area in the portrayal of the older characters in advertisements targeting the younger market is the positioning of the older person with others (see the first column of Table 10). The older individuals were positioned "With Other Adults" in the majority of advertisements in all three media (1) magazines, 50.0%; 2) newspapers, 61.1%; and 3) television, 51.9%). Placing the older individuals with other adults would be a situation where the "transgenerational approach" would be used (French & Fox, 1985, p. 62). Older characters shown interacting with other younger adults with the advertised products would make the products attractive to a variety of ages including the older market.

Overall, older characters in advertisements targeted at the younger audience were portrayed in a desirable manner, although the chances of an older character being portrayed in an undesirable manner were much greater when targeting the younger audience. In his content analysis of general interest magazines, Peterson (1992) found that in the advertisements specifically aimed at younger people the 65 and older group was shown desirable in 50% of the advertisements and undesirable in 50%. The present research found that the older characters received more minor and background roles, that 41.2% were portrayed in an undesirable manner, and that they were most often positioned with other adults. These findings support the past research in this area and provide a clear description of the portrayal of older individuals in advertisements targeting a younger audience.

Identifying the setting of the advertisement provides additional information on how the older characters are portrayed and any stereotypes associated with where an older person is placed in society. Research question six determines if the older character were placed in a home setting more than any other. "Home" represents, for the aged, a setting of confinement, refuge, solidarity, immobility, and boredom along with a feeling that they "don't get out much anymore" (Swayne & Greco, 1987, p. 53).

RQ 6: Do advertisements targeting the older audience show the older characters in a home setting?

The settings older characters were placed in are shown in Table 11.

Table 11: Settings in which the Older Characters Were Placed in Advertisements Targeting the Older Market

Setting of advertisement	Magazines n (%)	Newspapers n (%)	Television n (%)
Business	2 (4.9%)	0 (0.0%)	6 (6.5%)
Home	2 (4.9%)	10 (38.5%)	8 (8.7%)
Outdoors	28 (68.3%)	9 (34.6)	58 (63.0%)
Studio	3 (7.3%)	4 (15.4%)	15 (16.3%)
Other	6 (14.6%)	3 (11.5%)	5 (5.4%)
TOTAL (N)(%)	41 (100%)	26 (100%)	92 (100%)

Only newspapers had the largest percentage (38.5%) of older people appearing in a "Home" setting with "Outdoors" second at 34.6%. The "Outdoor" setting was the largest percentage in both magazines (68.3%) and television (63.0%). Sixty percent of the settings in all three media were "Outdoor" and only 12.6% of the characters were shown at "Home." These results indicate that when advertisers are targeting the older market they are not putting the older characters at home but outdoors in a more positive, active setting. Swayne and Greco (1987) found that 56% of the older individual on television commercials were in a home setting and Robinson et al. (1995) discovered that older individuals on prime-time television advertisements were shown most often outdoors (43.3%).

The research shows a positive trend in advertising of taking older people out of the home and putting them in a more active and healthy setting. Placing an older person in the park, on the porch, working in the garden or just outside enjoying nature is a very positive image for the older population.

The final research question takes into consideration all of the portrayal characteristics of the older individuals. The overall decision examined older people's 1) role, 2) how they were cast, 3) their physical, mental, and personality characteristics, 4) their placement with others, and 5) the setting in which they were placed to determine if the people were portrayed positively or negatively.

RQ7: Is there a difference in the overall portrayal of older individuals in the selected media?

The independent coders were also asked to evaluate the overall portrayal of the older characters as either "positive" (nonstereotyped) or "negative" (stereotyped) in each advertisement. The results are shown in Table 12. In all three media, and in all areas of targeting the overall portrayals are generally positive. Of the total of 682 older people in all of the advertisements, 85 (12.5%) were seen as being portrayed in a negative manner. In the advertisements targeted at the older market, 21.0% of the characters were negative and in the advertisements targeting the younger market 21.0% were negative. Having negative portrayals in advertisements targeting the younger audience was expected, but the 21% in advertisements targeting the older market is an area of major concern.   Even when the older market
is the target audience, 21% of the characters are portrayed in a stereotypical manner.

The number of health-related advertisements (43 or 67.2%, see Table 6) targeting the older market may be the reason for the numerous negative portrayals. The research shows, however, that older characters are continuing to be portrayed as sick, cranky, feeble, grouchy, slow, and having other negative characteristics. Most of the advertisements portray the older individuals in a positive manner, but as the results indicate there are areas where the image of older individuals can still be improved.

Table 12: Overall Portrayals of the Older Characters in Advertisements Targeting Each Market

MAGAZINES

Overall portrayal	Ads targeted toward under 49 n (%)	Ads targeted toward older market n (%)	Ads targeted toward all consumers n (%)
Positive	19 (86.4%)	39 (95.1%)	68 (98.6%)
Negative	3 (13.6%)	2 (4.9%)	1 (1.4%)
TOTAL (N)(%)	22 (100%)	41 (100%)	69 (100%)

NEWSPAPERS

Overall portrayal	Ads targeted toward under 49 n (%)	Ads targeted toward older market n (%)	Ads targeted toward all consumers n (%)
Positive	17 (94.4%)	23 (88.5%)	76 (93.8%)
Negative	1 (5.6%)	3 (11.5%)	5 (6.2%)
TOTAL (N)(%)	18 (100%)	26 (100%)	81 (100%)

TELEVISION

Overall portrayal	Ads targeted toward under 49 n (%)	Ads targeted toward older market n (%)	Ads targeted toward all consumers n (%)
Positive	101 (75.9%)	64 (69.6%)	190 (95.0%)
Negative	32 (24.1%)	28 (30.4%)	10 (5.0%)
TOTAL (N)(%)	133 (100%)	92 (100%)	200 (100%)

CHAPTER V

Summary and Conclusions

SUMMARY AND EXAMPLES

The overall driving objective of this study was to determine the degree to which certain advertisements in the media portray older individuals differently depending on the target audience. Specifically, this study examines marketers' and advertisers' attempts, in the electronic (e.g., television) and print (e.g., magazines and newspapers) media, to target and attract the business of the older American population.

Representation of Older Individuals

Older people appeared in 12% of all of the advertisements in the media studied, which is proportional to today's 13% older population in the United States. The actual number of older people in advertisements was, however, considerably lower than the older individuals present percentage of the population (13%). The underrepresentation of older individuals has been an area of concerns for the older population (Deets, 1994). A small number of older individuals in a high percentage of the studied advertisements indicates that when older people are placed in advertisements they are used alone or in small numbers. This research also shows that older characters are depicted alone most often in advertisements. The illusion that this type of representation and positioning creates is that older people are out there, but there just are not very many of them.

Only 5 out of every 100 people seen in the advertisements studied were age 65 or older. This 5% representation places the older population at a point of near nonexistence in advertising. Other researchers who found that the older population was underrepresented in advertising concluded the reason was that advertisers did not see the older population as major players in the consumer market (Gantz et al., 1980; Peterson, 1992; Robinson et al., 1995; Swayne & Greco, 1987). To determine if that conclusion was true, this study examined the percentage of advertisements, in the selected media, that targeted the older market.

Targeting the Older Market

When considering the fact that the older population in America is growing at such a rapid rate, has more disposable income, and has more free time than any other age demographic, aggressively targeting this group with products and services should be an obvious course for advertisers. The results of this study clearly indicate that the older market is being targeted in advertisements throughout the media. There were a total of 475 advertisements in all three media, and 84 (17.7%) were specifically targeted at the older market. Each of the three media also had high percentages (1) magazines, 22.5%; 2) newspapers, 16.9%; 3) television, 16.2%) indicating the wide use of the media to attract the business of the older market. The number of advertisements targeting the older market is greater than their percentage of the population. This finding is very positive for the older population. The results have shown that even though the number of older people in advertisements is low, the older market is being targeted through general interest media advertising. The marketers obviously see older consumers as potential buyers, but for what types of products?

Products Targeting the Older Market

The findings from this study indicate that an overwhelming majority (84.9%) of the current advertisements in the general interest media that target the older market are for products related to a person's health (e.g., medicine, health drinks, vitamins, health and life insurance, rest homes, funeral homes, etc.). The older population has expressed a concern that when they are the target market, the advertised product is usually health related (Festervand & Lumpkin, 1985). One example was for an advertisement for the Urology Center in southern Mississippi. The advertisement had a picture of an attractive older woman who seems to be happy with a headline that reads, "If someone you know suffers from loss of bladder control, finding a solution could be as simple as asking the right questions." With the picture and the topic together, this advertisement is obviously targeting the senior market. This topic is not one that people regularly choose to discuss in public, but older people are targeted for this kind of advertising reminding them of this potential or current medical problem.

The number of non-health related products in the media (15.1%) is low, especially when a number of companies have reported creating products and advertising campaigns specifically for the older market. If that is the case, they are not doing so in the general interest media advertisements (i.e., magazines, newspapers, and television). Certainly many of these companies place their advertisements in older related media such as magazines like *Modern Maturity* and *New Choices*. The results of this research have shown that product manufacturers, marketers, and advertisers are not utilizing the general interest media. Manufacturers of health-related products understand the need to advertise in the general interest media and are undoubtedly finding some success in doing so.

The discretionary incomes, active lifestyles, and the available time of the older market makes them the ideal target for "travel, leisure activities, personal-care products and services, leisure clothing, hobbies, sporting goods, health equipment, cosmetics, gardening equipment, food products, and active participation in community and nonprofit organizations" (Lazer, 1985, pp. 23-24). Two advertisements that effectively targeted the older market used the role of grandparent to sell their product and. The first was a television advertisement was for two children's games "Cootie" and "Don't Break the Ice." The advertisement shows a grandfather playing the games and laughing with his two grandchildren. The voice-over says: "Now you can share the fun of Cootie and Don't Break the Ice with your grandchildren." The second was a full-page public service announcement, for the Partnership for a Drug-Free America, published in the *New York Times* (1995). The advertisement had a picture of a grandfather holding his grandson and the copy read, "The power of Grandpa. Children have a very special relationship with Grandma and Grandpa. That's why grandparents can be such powerful allies in helping keep a kid off drugs." The advertisement continues by telling grandparents how they can become a bigger influence in their grandchildren's lives.

This research has shown that even though the total number of older individuals in media advertising is low, the older market is well represented in overall advertisements and advertisements that target their age demographic. The conclusion from past research, that marketers and advertisers do not see the older population as major players in the consumer market, has been supported by these findings. To better improve on the way a large, affluent, and growing group, such as the aged, is targeted, the total number of older people in advertisements should be increased. Additionally, marketers and advertisers need to begin aggressively marketing nonhealth-related products toward this group.

To better understand how older individuals are represented in media advertisements, their portrayal, in terms of their role, their casting, their mental, physical, and personality traits, and placement with others was determined. The advertisements were divided by target market to determine if older people are presented differently depending on who the advertisement was intended. When the advertisements with an older character were divided by target market, the results proved to be quite different.

Portrayal of Older Individuals in Media Advertisements Targeting the Older Market

In advertisements targeting the older market, older individuals were shown most often as "Active/Healthy" or "Happy/Content" and were cast as either a husband or a wife. For example, in an magazine advertisement for the medicine Zantac, published in *Reader's Digest*, a couple is shown sitting on a pier at a lake with their feet in the water having a picnic. The couple is smiling, playing in the water, and having a good time outdoors and being with each other. The makers of Zantac present the older couple in a positive manner because they want this desirable image to represent their product.

Another example of how older individuals are portrayed in a positive manner when they are the target market was in an advertisement for Nike Athletic Shoes. The advertisement was laid out in two pages and published in *Good Housekeeping* magazine. The headline in the advertisement read: "Beatrice Brophy, 72, and Barbara Anderson, 74, Canoeists and guides in the Boundary Waters of Minnesota." The two ladies are pictured smiling, having a good time, and carrying backpacks. The copy is written in free verse and describes growing old and the course that the characters' lives have taken. On the second page, there is a picture of a canoe with Nike's advertsing tag "Just Do It." Nike has run advertisements in the past targeting the older market and in each one they portray the older characters as healthy, active, and full of life. Nike is to be commended for their efforts in portraying older individuals in a positive manner and for reaching out, through this positive advertising, to older consumers who can still benefit from Nike products. More companies should follow Nike's lead in attempting to attract the business of the older market.

There are some advertisements that portrayed the older characters in an "undesirable" when the older market was the target. In addition to health problems, older people were often shown as lonely and sad. Festervand and Lumpkin (1985) found in their survey of older people that 50% believed they were shown in advertisements as "lonely." An advertisement for the Behavioral Healthcare Center in Hattiesburg, Mississippi, published in the *Hattiesburg American*, pictures an older woman looking at an old photo album with a lonely sad expression on her face. The headline read, "To everything there is a season. The transitions of life can be very difficult." What is projected in this advertisement is that older people, like the woman pictured, are sad, alone, and need help in dealing with the loss and loneliness in their lives.

Advertisers need to reevaluate the image of old age and older Americans when creating advertisements targeting the older market. Also, they need to look at the types of products that are targeting the older market and develop ways to use the general interest media as a means of attracting the business of the older market. The older market, because of their age, often need more health-related products than the young, but when these are the majority of products advertised to older Americans, then there is a problem. If advertisers and marketers continue to limit the products they advertise to this market and persist on using a negative image of aging then they risk the complete loss this important market, a market that will double in size as the baby boomers begin to reach maturity (Longino, 1994). As this growth takes place, America will see a group of older individuals who "have two or more incomes, multiple pensions, better retirement plans, better health, live longer, retire earlier and are more concerned with their quality of life" (Lazer & Shaw, 1987, p. 41). Eventually, marketers and advertisers will have to recognize the older market as serious consumers who purchase and use products and services, not because their health requires it, but because they have the time and money to enjoy them.

Portrayal of Older Individuals in Media Advertisements Targeting the Younger Market

Advertisements targeting the younger audience portray the older characters much differently from when the older market is the target. The older characters are given minor or background roles, are given undesirable characteristics, and are positioned mainly with other adults in the sample. In one advertisement for the television show "The Outer Limits," published in *TV Guide*, an older man is shown having a heart attack and a young doctor and nurse are trying to resuscitate him. In a similar type advertisement for American Medical Response, published in the *Sun Herald* newspaper in Gulfport, Mississippi, two young, strong Emergency Medical Technicians are shown standing in front of their ambulance. A smaller second picture on the left shows the EMTs placing an older woman into the ambulance. In both of these advertisements the older people play a minor role, are positioned with other adults, and are given the stereotypical characteristics of "Sick/Feeble." Using older individuals as patients indicates that marketers are continuing to use older individuals in stereotypical roles.

Another advertisement, published on the back cover of *Newsweek*, used a very positive picture of an older man, who seemed very happy and content with his life. But many times, it is not the picture that gave a negative portrayal, but the copy in the advertisement. The advertisement was for Cigna Retirement and Investment Services and the headline read simply, "Help." The copy in the advertisement said, "Mention retirement and what springs to mind? Fishing? You Wish. Try Working. Today, people are living longer, healthier lives. Which is wonderful, provided they have the means to enjoy it." Because this man has to work in his senior years he cannot enjoy his life. Statistics show that more older people today are working, not because they have to, but because they want to (Lazer, 1985).

Advertisements like the Cigna example were, however, the exception when the Younger market was the target. In other advertisements the older character was shown as a "Happy/Content" person and contributing to the scene. For example, in a Frigidaire advertisement, published in *Good Housekeeping*, shows a grandfather helping his grandson prepare lemonade to sell (see Appendix M). Also, on the back cover of the *National Geographic*, a Kodak advertisement has a grandmother graduating with her granddaughter hugging her (see

Appendix N). Both of these roles show the older person as a "happy grandparent," which is a positive portrayal of the older population.

CONCLUSIONS

The overall portrayal of the older Americans in this research was positive in all three media (1) magazines, 2) newspapers, and 3) television). There are still some problems, however, that need to be changed. More older characters, especially older females need to be used in advertising. There needs to be a better variety of products targeting the older market. When the older market is the target, the older characters should be shown without "sickness" and "disabilities." In advertisements targeting the younger audience, older characters need to be given more "Major" roles, and more "positive" characteristics.

By effectively targeting the older market, advertisers will find that this large, affluent, fast growing group will help increase their market share for many different products. To effectively target the older market, marketers need to better understand older individuals, who they are, their needs, wants, desires, what their likes and dislikes are, and what motivates them to buy a product. Marketers can also provide a positive social influence in their advertisements by accurately portraying older individuals. Younger individuals need to know that growing old does not mean that their lives are over and that older people can still contribute to society. Positive portrayals may also increase the self-image of older individuals who now see themselves in advertisements as "angry," "sick," and "unproductive."

LIMITATIONS OF STUDY

The present research discovered a small number of areas in the study that need to be addressed if the study is to be replicated or expanded. First, the sample of media (e.g., magazines, newspapers, and television) was limited not only in numbers but also by region. Choosing a larger sample of magazines, newspapers, and television time periods in addition to publication and broadcast in different areas of the United States may provide different results.

Second, the advertisements for movies, plays, and television programs provided a problem for categorizing the older actors. Deciding whether the actor should be coded as himself or herself (e.g., Clint Eastwood, Gene Hackman, Angela Lansberry) or as the character he or she is portraying in the program he or she is advertising. For example, does the coder categorize Matlock as the "Competent/ Intelligent" lawyer or Andy Griffith as the "Happy/Content" actor?

A third problem was the extensive use of photographs of people's heads in magazine and newspaper advertisements. For example, in newspapers a Realtor may have his or her picture next to a classified advertisement for a home. The problem that existed was there was no way to determine from the picture the person's role, how he or she was cast, how he or she was portrayed, the setting, or the overall portrayal. Advertisements for movies provided the same problem when only a picture of the actor was in the advertisement.

Fourth, the setting of "Home" and "Outdoors" presented a problem when the character was obviously shown outside of their home. For example, a couple sitting on the porch of their home is shown outside, yet still at the home. The operational definition of the "Home" setting for this study included only those settings that were inside the walls of the home. Everything outside the home was classified as "Outdoors." The problem with this is that even though the older person is outside their home they are still being portrayed as not getting out and contributing to society. Therefore, the "Outdoor" becomes misleading.

Finally, the fifth problem that existed was with the large number of individuals the coders classified as being between the age of 50 and 59. This group was, because of the operational definition of an older person, left out of the results. The number of individuals in this age group was not tabulated, but their use in advertisements targeting an older market was recorded (in magazines 27 times; in newspapers 3 times; in television 18 times). Because of their age and use in advertisements for the older market, these individuals should be included as part of the study. Additionally, the inclusion of individuals in their 50s in the results may help better define the use of older individuals in advertisements.

FUTURE RESEARCH

To provide a better understanding of the portrayal of older individuals in media advertisements, additional research is needed in several different areas. First, research needs to be conducted on how the older population perceive themselves in the media and how they believe marketers and advertisers are targeting them. This data will provide valuable information to marketers and researchers on how they can best attract the business of this valuable market. By comparing the beliefs of the older market to information from studies like the present one, marketers and advertisers can gauge how they are doing and develop ways to improve. Research in this area may also help marketers and advertisers decide the types of products to market toward older individuals and the most effective media to use.

Second, the perception older individuals have of their role in the "transgenerational approach" to advertising should be examined (French & Fox, 1985, p. 62). Does the inclusion of an older person in an advertisement mean that the older market is being targeted? If so, is the method effective, or if not, how could the method be improved so that the older market is targeted more? Research on the transgenerational approach, will require a survey of advertising agencies, marketers, and product manufacturers to determine the extent to which the method is used, how effective they believe the method to be, and ways, if any, they believe the method could be improved to include more older people.

Third, additional research is needed on the portrayal of older individuals in newspaper advertisements. Older people are the largest readers of newspapers in the United States and good quantitative and qualitative research on their portrayal in newspaper advertising is lacking in the discipline. A larger sample of newspapers and a bigger cross section of regional newspapers is needed to help understand how older people are used in this type of advertising. Also, the inserts, coupons, and weekly magazines (i.e., *USA Weekend*, *Parade*) in a newspaper should be examined to determine how the older market is used and targeted in these publications.

Fourth, research should be completed that examines the copy in advertisements that contain an older actor and those that target the older market. Smith (1976) found, in medical journal advertisements, even when the portrayal of the older characters was positive that the copy in the advertisements was generally negative. Shinar et al. (1980) also found that older characters were described in advertisements with negative attributes. Advertisers and marketers need to be aware that the image of older individuals includes not only their pictures but also what is said about them in the copy.

Fifth, additional research needs to be conducted on the influence advertising has on how older people view themselves in society. This issue is important because of the potential impact negative images in advertising may have on the cultivation of the older population. The cultivation theory, developed by Gerbner, Gross, Morgan, and

Signorielli (1994), decries the contribution the media have on the viewer and their view of social reality. Research needs to be conducted to determine if advertising in the media (i.e., magazines, newspapers, television) has an effect on the way older Americans see themselves. If negative images in advertising are found to contribute to a negative self-image, then advertisers and marketers can use that information to begin showing seniors as individuals who are capable, productive contributors to society.

Finally, the research on cultivation theory needs to be extended to younger audiences to determine the influence media advertisements have on their perception of older people and growing old. Gerbner et al. (1980) state that "Images of old age cultivate our concept of aging and the age roles we assume" (p. 37). Negative portrayals of older individuals in advertisements may influence young people to dread growing old and form the belief that when they are old their lives are over. In their study of television dramas, Gerbner et al. discovered that young people who were heavy viewers of television perceived old people in "generally negative terms" (p. 46). Research on the cultivation of advertising would indicate the influence, if any, advertising images have on the younger people of society.

Continuing to conduct quality research on the uses, portrayal, and cultivation of advertising will assist scholars in comprehending the older market. Research in this area is vital for marketers and advertisers as they develop products, services, and advertising that will attract the rapidly growing older market. But to be effective, much work remains to be done.

Appendices

APPENDIX A: TOTAL NUMBER ADVERTISEMENTS

Magazine	Total number of advertisements	Total number of ads with an older person	Percentage
TV Guide	224	22	9.8%
Ladies Home Journal	183	8	4.4%
Good Housekeeping	164	8	4.9%
McCall's	143	7	4.9%
Better Homes & Gardens	134	10	7.5%
Reader's Digest	85	24	28.2%
Family Circle	78	3	3.9%
Time	49	10	20.4%
National Geographic	40	3	7.5%
Newsweek	39	7	18.0%
TOTAL (N)(%)	1,139	102	9.0%

Newspaper	Total number of advertisements	Total number of ads with an older person	Percentage
New York Times	506	44	8.7%
Mobile Press Register	131	10	7.6%
Clarion Ledger	100	7	7.0%
Sun Herald	81	7	8.6%
Times Picayune	78	6	7.7%
Wall Street Journal	70	6	8.6%
Hattiesburg American	58	4	6.8%
USA Today	57	5	8.8%
TOTAL (N)(%)	1,081	89	8.2%

APPENDIX A: TOTAL NUMBER ADVERTISEMENTS cont.

Television Network	Total number of advertisements	Total number of ads with an older person	Percentage
CBS	462	84	18.2%
ABC	456	85	18.6%
FOX	445	59	13.3%
NBC	407	56	13.8%
TOTAL (N)(%)	1,770	284	16.1%

APPENDIX B: TOTAL NUMBER OF PEOPLE IN ADVERTISEMENTS

Magazine	Total number of advertisements	Total number of ads with an older person	Percentage
TV Guide	667	30	4.5%
Good Housekeeping	321	8	2.5%
Ladies Home Journal	261	9	3.5%
Better Homes & Gardens	253	10	4.0%
McCall's	224	7	3.1%
Reader's Digest	183	37	20.2%
Family Circle	129	5	3.9%
National Geographic	109	4	3.7%
Time	93	14	15.1%
Newsweek	62	8	13.0%
TOTAL (N)(%)	2,302	132	5.7%

Newspaper	Total number of advertisements	Total number of ads with an older person	Percentage
New York Times	1208	62	5.1%
Mobile Press Register	330	15	4.6%
Sun Herald	287	10	3.5%
USA Today	186	7	3.8%
Clarion Ledger	174	9	5.2%
Wall Street Journal	167	8	4.8%
Times Picayune	166	9	5.4%
Hattiesburg American	120	5	4.2%
TOTAL (N)(%)	2,638	125	4.7%

APPENDIX B: TOTAL NUMBER OF PEOPLE IN ADVERTISEMENTS cont.

Television Network	Total number of advertisements	Total number of ads with an older person	Percentage
FOX	2,232	78	3.5%
ABC	2,147	121	5.6%
NBC	1,903	123	6.5%
CBS	1,596	103	6.5%
TOTAL (N)(%)	7,878	425	5.5%

Glossary

Advertising—Any paid form of targeted communication about an organization, product, service, or idea by an identified sponsor presented through the mass media (Belch & Belch, 1994; DeFleur & Dennis, 1991). For this study, the advertising will be limited to print advertisements in magazines and newspapers and broadcast advertisements on television.

Character Portrayals—Whom the actor is representing or what part he or she is playing in the advertisement will be considered as part of his or her character portrayal. The character portrayals may be one of, but not limited to, the following:

Husband/Wife—The "Husband/Wife" portrayal is a person shown in the advertisement with a spouse or one who appears to be with a spouse. To be classified as a husband or wife there must be a couple in the advertisement. An older couple, of the same age, where there was an obvious family relationship or physical contact would be considered a Husband/Wife. For example a woman and man sitting on a park bench holding hands would be classified as a Husband/Wife.

Parent—The "Parent" portrayal is an older person who is shown with a middle-aged person in a family situation. A home setting, physical contact or relationship, and shown respect, in addition to what was said in the advertisement determined if a person was cast as a Parent.

Grandparent—The "Grandparent" portrayal is an older person shown with a child or young adult in a family situation. A home setting, physical contact or relationship, and shown respect, in addition to what was said in the advertisement determined if a person was cast as a Grandparent.

Owner/Boss—The "Owner/Boss" portrayal is a person who obviously owns the business in the advertisement (e.g., Dave Thomas from Wendy's or car dealers who are their own spokesperson) or a person cast as the boss of the particular business. The business owner or boss is distinguished by having employees or people working for him or her.

Worker/Employee—The "Worker/Employee" portrayal is a person working at a place of business where they are helping customers or serving others. Wal-Mart and McDonald's both have advertisements where older employees are shown helping customers. The worker/employee character is not the boss or in charge of the company but rather works for someone else.

Consumer—The "Consumer" portrayal is a person who is shopping, purchasing, or using the product in the advertisement. A store or home setting will be key to determining if the person is a consumer. Individuals shown buying a product in the store would be considered a consumer and also individuals shown using the product. For example, a person driving the advertised car or painting with the advertised paint would be characterized as a consumer.

General Interest Media—Magazines, newspapers, and television that are popular with a variety of different audience members constitute the general interest media. General interest media is not specific in their targeting, and while some may be designed for a specific group, the media is available for all members of society. Television is the best example of a medium that attracts the mass audience through general interest programming. Pember (1983) describes the general interest media as having, "vast circulation, fascinating content, a modicum of public service, lots of advertising, and low prices" (p. 40).

Local Advertisements—Belch and Belch (1995) define local advertising as "advertising done by companies within the limited geographical area where they do business. Examples of local advertisers include hospitals, grocery stores, Realtors, and insurance salespeople.

Marketer—The marketer is the manager of the marketing plan. Marketing is defined by The American Marketing Association as "the process of planning and executing the conception, pricing, promotion, and distribution of ideas, goods, and services, to create exchanges that satisfy individual and organizational objectives" (Belch & Belch, 1994, p. 6). Examples of a marketer would be Procter & Gamble, General Mills, and the Coca-Cola Company.

Media—Sometimes referred to as mass media, media are defined as the devices for "moving messages across distance or time to accomplish mass communication. The major mass media in modern society are books, magazines, newspapers, motion pictures, radio, and television" (DeFleur & Dennis, 1991, p. 22). This study will concentrate on the advertisements in magazines (e.g., *Newsweek*, *Time*, & *Reader's Digest*) and newspapers (e.g., *New York Times*, *USA Today*, and *Wall Street Journal*), and on television (e.g., commercial networks ABC, CBS, FOX, & NBC).

National Advertising—According to Belch and Belch (1995) national advertising is "advertising done by a company on a nationwide basis or in most regions of the country and targeted to the ultimate consumer market" (p. 714). Examples of national advertisers include Ford, General Electric, McDonald's, Taco Bell, and Visa.

Older Individuals—German Chancellor Otto Von Bismarck has been credited with establishing the age of 65 as the minimum age for a person to retire in the 1880s (Morgan, 1991). Today, Government statistical reports and the U.S. Department of Health and Human Services continue to define senior citizens as those 65 years of age and older (Healthy People 2000, 1992). Those in the medical profession agree that 75 is the age when the body becomes vulnerable to human frailties (Linden, 1985). Scholars conducting research on older adults and the media use the age of 65 as the determining age for when a person is considered to be old (Cassata, Anderson & Skill, 1980; Davis & Kubey, 1982; Northcott, 1975; Gantz et at. 1980; Lazer, 1985; Lazer & Shaw, 1987; Linden, 1986; Milliman & Erffmeyer, 1990; Peterson, 1992; Swayne & Greco, 1987). Others use an age of 50 to 55 to describe an older individual (Bell, 1992; Hiemstra, Goodman, Middlemiss, Vosco & Ziegler, 1983) which may agree with marketers who believe "that 50 is the line that divides older consumer from the rest of the population" (Linden, 1985, p. 43). The presence of an older person in these studies is determined by the use of subjective criteria such as the appearance of retirement, extensive gray hair, wrinkles of the skin around the eyes and/or hands, use of aids such as canes or wheelchairs, the parent of a son or daughter who was middle-aged or older, or evidence of grandchildren or great-grandchildren in addition to chronological age (Gantz et al., 1980; Peterson, 1992; Swayne & Greco, 1987)

Needless to say, defining the older population is a difficult task. The *Dictionary of Gerontology* defines an older person as "an individual who is age 65 or older. An older person is defined in modern Western societies in terms of chronological age (the number of years a person has lived)" (Harris, 1988, p.129). Older people are divided into three different demographic groups, 1) the young-old (age 65 to 74), 2) the old-old (age 75 to 84), and 3) the oldest-old (age 85 and older) (Harris, 1988, p. 130). This study operationally defines an older person as someone who is chronologically age 65 or older.

In addition to the chronological age, the terminology used to describe older individuals must be determined. In the past, researchers have referred to the 65 and older group as "elderly" (Abrams, 1981; Bell, 1992; Davis & Davis, 1985; Festervand & Lumpkin, 1985; Gantz et al., 1980; Gorn, Goldberg, Chattopadhyay, & Litvack, 1991; Greco, 1988; Greco & Swayne, 1992; Moore & Cadeau, 1985; Longino, 1994; Lumpkin & Hite, 1988; Lutsky, 1980; Mares & Cantor, 1992; Meeks, 1994; Morgan, 1991; Korzenny & Neuendorf, 1980; Robinson, Duet, & Smith, 1995; Schreiber & Boyd, 1980; Smith, 1976; Ursic, Ursic, & Ursic, 1986), "aged" (Davis & French, 1989), "seniors" (Milliman & Erffmeyer, 1989), "senior citizens" (Peterson, 1992), and "older Americans, adults, consumers, or people" (Cassata, Anderson, & Skill, 1980; Hiemstra et al., 1983; Hitschler, 1993; Lazer & Shaw, 1987; Linden, 1985; Meeks, 1992; Swayne & Greco, 1987).

Other terms for the older population include "golden-ager" (Harris, 1988, p. 129); "senescent" (Kalish, 1975); "gray" (Konrad & DeGeorge, 1989, p. 64); "mature" (Deets, 1993, p. 134; Lazer, 1985, p. 23); "muppies" (mature urban professionals) (Lehrer, 1991, p. 13); "seasoned citizens" (Limbaugh, 1992) and "geriatrics" (Harris, 1988, p. 129). The *Publication Manual of the American Psychological Association* (1994) states that the term "elderly" is not acceptable as a noun and should be replaced with "older person." The American Association of Retired Persons (AARP) does not use the term "elderly" and prefers that their members be refered to as "older Americans" or "older people" (p. 53). Therefore, "older" or "aged" will be the terms used to refer to those individuals 65 years of age or older.

Other Markets—For this study, other markets include all target markets except the older market (e.g., children, adolescents, young adults, and adults 18 to 49 years of age).

Overall Portrayal—The overall portrayal describes the how the actor was seen in each advertisement when all areas (role, type of character, physical, mental, or personality traits, and setting) are considered. The overall portrayal is limited to the following:

Positive Overall Portrayal—In a "Positive" overall portrayal the older character is shown in desirable manner. The Positive portrayal is one that is free from negative stereotypes such as showing the older person as a "sufferer in need of laxatives, denture adhesives, or sleeping pills" (Abrams, 1981, p. 27) or "cranky," "sick," "decrepit," or "senile," (Davis & Davis, 1985). The older person was shown as active, healthy, happy, working and contributing to society in a Positive portrayal. Deciding if the portrayal is "Positive" the person would ask "Is this how I would like to be portrayed in an advertisement?"

Negative Overall Portrayal—The "Negative" portrayal is the opposite of the Positive portrayal. The older character is seen in a stereotypical manner (e.g., sick, feeble, confused, grouchy, etc.) and as an undesirable character. The same question, "Would I like to be portrayed like this in an advertisement?" would be asked by the person deciding if the portrayal is Negative. In this case, however, the response would be "no."

Physical, Mental, or Personality Traits of Characters—The personality and physical traits that describe the type of person the actor is portraying in the advertisement will be considered here. These traits may include, but not limited to, any of the following:

Active/Healthy—When the person in the advertisement was involved with an activity that required physical activity and a healthy body he or she wwas classified as "Active/Healthy." Characters who were shown jogging, working out, playing golf, or participating in other physical activities were classified as Active/Healthy. For example, in an advertisement for NordicTrack (a physical fitness equipment manufacturer) an older actor wass shown in a number of their advertisements using their workout machine.

Sick/Feeble—When a person was shown in poor health he or she was considered "Sick/Feeble." The setting was important in determining if someone was sick. Being in bed, lying down, in a hospital or institution, at the doctor's office all indicated sickness. In addition, signs of sickness in personal appearance (e.g., redness of face, swollen eyes, stuffy head, etc.) and what was said in the advertisement were used to identify illness. To determine if a person was feeble, physical signs such as lack of mobility, frailty, using a cane, walker or wheelchair, or being nonresponsive to their environment was used to recognize this characteristic.

Competent/Intelligent—When a person was cast as a doctor, scientist, teacher, or a person of knowledge, he or she was considered "Competent/Intelligent." While many characters were seen as having intelligence, this personality trait took into account the overall role of the character. For example, a man shown in a laboratory, wearing a lab coat, recommending the use of Tylenol for the flu would be considered Competent/Intelligent. In addition to his or her professional position, this person was in charge of the situation in the advertisement and would normally be an advice giver.

Humorous/Comical—When a person was given a humorous role in which his or her character was the one responsible for making the advertisement funny. The character's dress, demeanor, personality, and mental state was considered when deciding if the character was "Humorous/Comical." For example, many of the Little Caesars advertisements cast older characters in humorous roles.

Sexy/Macho—When a person was placed in an advertisement with the intention of looking or acting desirable he or she was classified as "Sexy/Macho." Personal appearance, dress, and what was said in the advertisement were considered here. For example, Nike ran a television commercial with older individuals running, working out, and lifting weights. One of the males was shown without his shirt, pumping iron and flexing his muscles. This character would be considered Sexy/Macho.

Angry/Disgruntled—When a person was seen as mean, grouchy, irritable, or grumpy he or she was classified as "Angry/Disgruntled." Facial expressions, body language, demeanor, and what was said in the advertisement were considered when deciding if a person was Angry/Disgruntled. A person that ass irritated about a situation would be classified here but a person who was sad or sorrowful was not. For example, in a Mercury Villager advertisement the owner of a competitive car manufacturer was shown through his facial expressions and body language to be upset that their minivan was not of the same quality as the Mercury Villager. This person would be considered Angry/Disgruntled.

Happy/Content—When a person was shown enjoying the situation in the advertisement he or she was considered "Happy/Content." Smiling, cheerful, relaxed, and peaceful would all be characteristics of a Happy/Content person. For example, in the Werther's Candy advertisement a grandfather shown hugging his grandson with a smile on his face would be considered Happy/Content.

Placement of the Older Person with Others—The placement with others describes who the older person was with in the advertisement. The placement with others may include, but is not limited to, any of the following:

Alone—When an older person is the single participant in an advertisement he or she will be classified "Alone." Situations where there is a married couple (husband and wife) by themselves will also be included in this category to indicate that the couple was portrayed alone. For example, a husband and wife sitting on a porch swing, with no other people around, would be seen as a couple (or alone) as opposed to being categorized as "All Older People."

With All Older People—Older individuals will be classified in this category when they are in an advertisement with other individuals their same age (65 or older). For example, a group of older people sitting around the table playing cards and discussing the kinds of life insurance they have would be a situation where each older woman would positioned "With All Older People."

With Other Adults—Older people placed in the advertisement with individuals who are not children (preteen) and not older (65 or older) are considered "With Other Adults." Examples would include an older woman pictured working in the garden with her middleaged daughter, or an older man buying a television from a middleaged sales clerk.

With Children Only—This type of placement is when an older person is shown in the advertisement with only children (preteen). One example of the "With Children Only" placement is in a Werther's Candy advertisement where a grandfather is shown sharing his candy with his grandson. Here the only two characters in the advertisements are the grandfather and his grandson.

With Mixed Ages—Advertisements that have the older characters with a mixture of other adults, children, and other older people is considered "With Mixed Ages." For example, a Kodak Film advertisement picturing a family with individuals from three generations would have the grandparents positioned With Mixed Ages.

Portrayal—The portrayal is the role, the type of character the actor plays, how the character's personality, physical, and mental state is shown, the older person's placement with others, what type of setting the older characters are placed in, and what the overall portrayal of the character is in each advertisement.

Roles—A role is the part that the actor plays in the advertisement. Actors will either be the main character or play some other supporting part in the advertisement. The definition of the major, minor and background roles was taken from Swayne and Greco (1987) and Robinson, Duet, and Smith (1995), who found that these categories were an effective way to determine the use of the older actors. The major, minor, and background roles are defines as follows:

Major Role—The major role includes all people on camera who speak or have a dominant part throughout the advertisement, or is the main character in the advertisement (e.g., Dave for Wendy's, James Whitmore for Miracle Gro).

Minor Role—The minor role includes individuals who are on camera for less than one half of the advertisement, or play a supporting role.

Background Role—The background role includes individuals who do not speak or are seen in the advertisement only briefly. Crowd scenes, camera scans of a restaurant or park where people are present, but not involved any more than an inanimate object used to develop the scene, were considered background roles.

Settings—The setting describes the place or situation the actor is in during the advertisement. These settings may include, but are not limited to, any of the following:

Business/Work—The "Business/Work" setting is when the older person is seen in his or her place of business, work, or at the company in which he or she owns or operates. Wal-Mart has a series of advertisements showing their employees hard at work in the stores. Dave Thomas for Wendy's is often working in the kitchen or behind the counter of one of his restaurants. Also, business people shown in an office or in a work environment would be in a Business/Work setting.

Home—The "Home" is when an individual is pictured in the living room, kitchen, bedroom, or other room in the house. Settings outside the home (e.g., yard, garden, or porch) would not be included in the Home setting and would be placed in a different setting (i.e., "Outdoors"). The Home setting is restricted to the confines of the walls in a house.

Outdoors—The "Outdoor" setting is all settings that are outside and free from any kind of shelter (i.e., home). The park, a garden, the ocean, the porch, etc., are all examples of the Outdoor setting. A couple riding bicycles in the park would be Outdoors, but a man clipping roses in a greenhouse would not.

Studio—The "Studio" setting includes those situations where the characters are in an artificial setting. Advertisements in a room with background lighting, props, and sets would be in a Studio. In a Publisher's Clearing House advertisements, Ed McMahan is shown walking in a room with the pictures of the past winners on the walls and spotlights hitting the pictures would be an example of a Studio setting.

Stereotyping—The Gray Panthers, a group actively fighting against "ageist portrayals" of older individuals in all areas of the media (i.e., magazines, newspapers, radio, television, etc.), define stereotyping as

> something conforming to a fixed or general pattern; a standardized
> mental picture that is held in common by members of a group and

that represents an oversimplified opinion or uncritical judgment. Stereotypes are exaggerated beliefs about a specific group, usually based on misconceptions, prejudgment, or over categorization. (Gray Panthers, 1983, pp. 1 & 7)

Common stereotypes of older individuals include showing them sitting in a rocking chair watching life go by, staying home, being sick, decrepit, senile, or grouchy.

Targeting—The process of directing advertising and promotion to a fraction of all consumers that constitutes the prime prospects or target market for the product or service (Weilbacher, 1984). The following target markets were examined in this study:

Under 18 years of age—Products such as video games, breakfast cereals, candy, and toys have advertisements specifically designed to attract children and teens. The age of the characters, specific reference to age, and the type of product will determine if the product is targeting the under 18 market. An example of this type of product is the advertisements for Trix cereal with the famous slogan, "Silly rabbit, Trix are for kids."

18 to 49 years old—Advertisements considered to be targeting the 18 to 49 age demographic must have a specific reference, either verbal or visual, to this audience. In addition to age, the references associated with this audience may include activities (e.g., Mountain Dew's campaign with people in their 20s sky diving, mountain biking, and skiing), a way of life (e.g., Ford Aerostar Mini Van commercials show a mother with small children), or a position in society (e.g., Campbell's Soup advertises to college students).

Older Market—Because the ages of 18 to 49 have been determined as an age that advertisers target their products (Castro, 1989; Seligson, 1993; Taylor, 1995), the "Older Market" consists of products targeted toward individuals older than 49 which includes the older demographic (e.g., individuals age 65 and older). Advertisements considered to be targeting the older market must have a specific reference, either verbal or visual, to this audience. In addition to age, references made about a way of life (e.g., retired, senior life), a position in a family (e.g., grandparent, great aunt or uncle), or and advertisement with all older characters will assist in determining if the older market is the target audience. For example, Centrum Silver is advertised as a vitamin for seniors, the actors are all older individuals, and the copy in the advertisements that the product is for individuals in their senior years.

All Consumers—Advertisements without a specific reference to age or an age demographic are considered targeting "All Consumers." Products and advertisements are not specifically designed to appeal to all audiences, but at the same time they do not exclude any particular age group. Advertisements for Wal-Mart, Sears, JCPenney, and Wendy's all have advertising campaigns that do not exclude any age group. The popularity of the "transgenerational approach" in advertising, where all age groups are represented, attracts not only the older audience but the mass population as well (French & Fox, 1985, p. 62).

Bibliography

Abrams, B. (1981, March 5). Advertisers start recognizing cost of insulting the elderly. *Wall Street Journal, 942*(44), 27.

Bell, J. (1992). In search of a discourse on aging: The elderly on television. *The Gerontologist, 32*,(3), 305-311.

Cassata, M. B., Anderson, P. A., & Skill, T. D. (1980). The older adult in daytime serial drama. *Journal of Communication, 30*, 48-49.

Castro, J. (1989, March 6). Is that you on TV grandpa? *Time, 139*, 53.

Crispell, D., & Frey, W. H. (1993) American maturity. *American Demographics, 15*(3), 31-42.

Davis, B., & W. A. French (1989). Exploring advertising usage segments among the aged. *Journal of Advertising Research, 29*(1), 22-29.

Davis, R. H. (1975). Television and the image of aging. *Television Quarterly, 12*, 21-24.

Davis, R. H., & Davis, J. A. (1985). *TV's image of the elderly*. Lexington, KY: Lexington Books.

Davis, R. H., & Kubey, R. W. (1982). Growing old on television and with television. In D. Pearl, L. Bouthilet, & J. Lazer (Eds.), *Television and behavior: Vol. II. Ten years of scientific progress and implications for the eighties* (pp. 201-208). Rockville, MD: U.S. Department of Health and Human Services, National Institute of Mental Health.

Deets, H. B. (1993, December 15). The media and the mature marketplace. *Vital Speeches of the Day, 60*, 134-136.

DeFleur, M. L., & Dennis, E. E. (1991). *Understanding mass communication*. Boston: Houghton Mifflin.

Diamond, E., & Ohringer, M. (1993, April). CBS: Why it may be the only network for us. *New Choices, 33*, 34-37

Doka, K. J. (1992, July/August). When gray is golden: Business in an aging America. *The Futurist, 26,* 16-20.

Festervand, T. A., & Lumpkin, J. R. (1982). Response of elderly consumers to their portrayal by advertisers. In J. H. Leigh & C. R. Martin (Eds.), *Current issues and research in advertising* (pp. 203-226). Ann Arbor, MI: Graduate School of Business Administration, University of Michigan.

Foote, K. A. (1994/95). The aging population. *Issues in Science and Technology, 11,* 80-81.

French, W A., & Fox, R. (1985). Segmenting the senior citizen market. *Journal of Consumer Marketing, 2,* 61-74.

Gantz, W., Gartenberg, H. M., & Rainbow, C. K. (1980). Approaching invisibility: The portrayal of the elderly in magazine advertisements. *Journal of Communication, 30,* 56-60.

Gerbner, G., Gross, L., Signorielli, N., & Morgan, M. (1980). Aging with television: Images on television drama and conceptions of social reality. *Journal of Communication, 30,* 37-47.

Gerbner, G., Gross, L., Signorielli, N., & Morgan, M. (1994). Growing up with television: The cultivation perspective. In J. Bryant & D. Zillmann (Eds.), *Media effects: Advances in theory and research* (pp. 17-41). Hillsdale, NJ: Erlbaum.

Gorn, G. J., Goldberg, M. E., Chattopadhyay, A., & Litvack, D. (1991). Music and information in commercials: Their effects with an elderly sample. *Journal of Advertising, 20*(3), 23-32.

Greco, A. J. (1988). The elderly as communicators: Perceptions of advertising practitioners. *Journal of Advertising Research, 28*(3), 39-46.

Hanson, P. (1987, April 16). *Psychographic and lifestyle perspectives on the senior market.* Paper presented to the Marketing to the Senior Segment: The Health and Lifestyles of America's Aging Population Conference, Louisville, KY.

Harris, A. J., & Feinberg, J. F. (1977). Television and aging: Is what you see what you get? *The Gerontologist, 17* (5), 464-468.

Harris, D. K. (1988). *Dictionary of gerontology.* Westport, CT: Greenwood Press.

Hiemstra, R., Goodman, M., Middlemiss, M. A., Vosco, R., & Ziegler, N. (1983). How older persons are portrayed in television advertising: Implications for educators. *Educational Gerontology, 9*(2-3), 111-122.

Hitschler, P. B. (1993). Spending by older consumers: 1980 and 1990 compared. *Monthly Labor Review, 111,* 3-13.

Holsti, O. (1969). *Content analysis for the social sciences and humanities.* Reading, MA: Addison-Wesley.

Kalish, R. A. (1975). *Late adulthood: Perspectives on human development*. Monterey, CA: Brooks/Cole.

Kassarjian, H. H. (1977). Content analysis in consumer research. *Journal of Consumer Research, 4*, 8 -18.

Konrad, W., & DeGeorge, G. (1989, April 3). U.S. companies go for the gray. *Business Week*, 64-67.

Korzenny, F. & Neuendorf, K.(1980). Television viewing and self-concept of the elderly. *Journal of Communication, 30*, 71-88.

Kubey, R. W. (1980). Television and aging: Past, present, and future. *The Gerontologist, 20*(1), 16-35.

Lazer, W. (1985). Inside the mature market. *American Demographics, 7*(3), 48-49.

Lazer, W., & Shaw, E. H. (1987). How older Americans spend their money. *American Demographics, 9*(9), 36-41.

Lehrer, S. (1991, April). Marketing to muppies pays off. *USA Today, 119*, 13.

Limbaugh, R. (1992). *The way things ought to be.* New York: Simon & Schuster, Inc.

Linden, F. (1985, July/August). New money and the old. *Across the Board*, 43-48.

Longino, C. F. Jr., (1994, December). The new elderly: Myths of an aging population. *Current, 368*, 22-24.

Lumpkin, J. R., & Hite, R. E. (1988). Retailers' offerings and elderly consumers' needs: Do retailers understand the elderly? *Journal of Business Research, 16*, 313-326.

Lutsky, N. S. (1980). Attitudes toward old age and elderly persons. In C. Eisdorfer (Ed.), *Annual review of gerontology and geriatrics* (pp. 287-336). New York: Springer.

Mares, M. L., & Cantor, J. (1992). Elderly viewer's response to televised portrayals of old age. *Communication Research, 19*(4), 459-478.

McTavish, D. G. (1971). Perceptions of old people: A review of research methodologies and findings. *Gerontologist, 11*, 98-101.

Meeks, C. B. (1994). Technological change and the elderly. *Advancing the Consumer Interest, 6*(1), 15-20.

Milliman, R. E., & Erffmeyer, R. C. (1990). Improved advertising aimed at seniors. *Journal of Advertising Research, 29*(6), 31-36.

Moore, T. E., & Cadeau, L. (1985). The representation of women, the elderly and minorities in Canadian television commercials. *Canadian Journal of Behavioral Science, 17*(3), 215-225.

Morgan C. L. (1991, June). Economic impact of the elderly not always a boon. *Farmline, 12*(6), 12-14.

Northcott, H. C. (1975). Too young, too old — age in the world of television. *The Gerontologist, 15*(2), 184-186.

Peterson, R. T. (1992). The depiction of senior citizens in magazine advertisements: a content analysis. *Journal of Business Ethics, 11*(9), 701-706.

Robinson II, T. E., Duet, R., & Smith, T. V. (1995). The elderly in advertising: A content analysis of prime-time television commercials. In: *Proceedings of the 1995 Conference of the American Academy of Advertising* (pp. 1-11).

Rosencranz, H., & McNevin, T. A. (1969). Factor analysis of attitudes toward the aged. *The Gerontologist, 9*(1), 55-59.

Schick, F. L. (1986). *Statistical handbook on aging Americans.* Phoenix, AZ: Oryx Press.

Schreiber, E. S., & Boyd, D. A. (1980). How the elderly perceive television commercials. *Journal of Communication, 30*(1), 61-70.

Seligson, M. (1993, March). Us? Weak consumers? You've gotta be kidding! *New Choices, 33*, 44-46.

Shaw R. (1993, July 19). Graying and green. *Mediaweek,* 20-24.

Shinar, D., Tomer, A., & Biber, A. (1980). Images of old age in televised dramas imported to Israel. *Journal of Communication, 30*, 50-55.

Simmons Market Research Bureau, Inc. (1994). *Simmons 1994 study of media and markets,* New York, NY.

Smith, M. C. (1976). Portrayal of the elderly in prescription drug advertising. *The Gerontologist, 16*(4), 329-334.

Standard Rate and Data Service (1984). *Consumer magazine and agri-media rates and data.* Wilmette, IL: Macmillan.

Swayne, L. E., & Greco, A. J. (1987). The portrayal of old Americans in television commercials. *Journal of Advertising, 16*(1), 48-54.

Taylor, S. C. (1995, November-December). Primetime's big sleep. *Modern Maturity,* 38-43.

Ursic, A. C., Ursic, M. L., & Ursic, V. (1986). A longitudinal study of the uses of the elderly in magazine advertising. *Journal of Consumer Research, 13*, 131-133

Weilbacher, W. M. (1984). *Advertising* (2nd ed.). New York: MacMillan.

Wimmer, R. D. & Dominick, J. R. (1991). *Mass media research, an introduction.* Belmont, CA: Wadsworth.

Wyatt, J. (1995, February 6). Playing the woofie card. *Fortune, 131*, 130-132.

Index